Saint Edith Stein

Saint Edith Stein

A Spiritual Portrait

Dianne Marie Traflet

BOOKS & MEDIA

Boston

Library of Congress Cataloging-in-Publication Data

Traflet, Dianne Marie.
   Saint Edith Stein : a spiritual portrait / by Dianne M. Traflet.
      p. cm.
   Includes bibliographical references.
   ISBN 0-8198-7108-7 (pbk.)
   1. Stein, Edith, Saint, 1891–1942. 2. Carmelite Nuns—
Germany—Biography. 3. Philosophers—Germany—Biography.
4. Spiritual biography. I. Title.
   BX4705.S814T73 2008
   282.092—dc22

                                        2008014551

Cover design by Rosana Usselmann

Cover photo from the Edith Stein Archive at the Carmelite Monastery at Cologne, Germany. Used with permission.

Interior photos from The Edith Stein Archive at the Carmelite Monastery at Cologne, Germany. Used with permission.

"P" and PAULINE are registered trademarks of the Daughters of St. Paul.

Published by Pauline Books & Media, 50 Saint Paul's Avenue, Boston, MA 02130-3491

Printed in the U.S.A.

www.pauline.org

Pauline Books & Media is the publishing house of the Daughters of St. Paul, an international congregation of women religious serving the Church with the communications media.

2 3 4 5 6 7 8 9   19 18 17 16 15

Dedicated to
those with whom I have been privileged to pray and work,
and to the administration, faculty, students, and staff of:

Immaculate Conception Seminary School of Theology
Seton Hall University
Archdiocese of Newark, New Jersey

St. John Fisher Seminary
Diocese of Bridgeport, Connecticut

Brandsma Priory
Carmelite Novitiate
Middletown, New York

St. Andrew's College Seminary
Seton Hall University

Assumption College for Sisters
Mallinkrodt Convent
Mendham, New Jersey

Contents

Introduction:
The Challenge of Beginnings

Edith Stein would have known how to begin this book. She was a beginner par excellence. A brilliant writer, speaker, and philosopher, Edith was a woman of exceptional accomplishments precisely because she had mastered the art of beginning. Indeed, she started her voluminous work, *Finite and Eternal Being*, with these words: "This book was written by a beginner for beginners." In a spirit of humility, she was referring primarily to her intellectual growth in the field of philosophy, as she explained: "At an age when others may confidently call themselves teachers, the author was compelled to start over again."[1] If Edith had written a book describing her journey in the spiritual life, she likely would have begun in the same way, emphasizing her role as a beginner and her appreciation for the opportunities to "start over again." Edith realized that the spiritual journey is for novices, those who never stop pondering, searching, and discovering. It is for those who do not fear to become experts in humility. Such beginners advance only after they realize that they might fall again, even repeatedly, or they may hit a roadblock. They recognize that to walk in the light, they first must stumble in the dark. Such beginners realize that their journey often demands that they pause before detours and stop signs. When their pace is too quick, they realize they need to slow down and sometimes start again. They begin anew, open to a change in direction and the possibility of awe-inspiring discoveries. With each new path, they become more childlike, more willing to let go of their well-worn routines, detailed maps, and definitive plans. Life becomes an adventure.

This woman of great success and great love lived an adventure in humility. She fearlessly became childlike, allowing God to take the lead, to introduce her to uncharted paths. "Basically," she said, "it is always a small, simple truth that I have to express: *How to go about living at the Lord's hand.*"[2] She expressed that truth passionately, not only in her lectures and writings, but also in the sorrows, joys, and challenges of her everyday life.

Edith learned to recognize the gentleness of God's whispers and the strength of his voice leading her along the adventure of life. What she heard, she followed. With trust, she was content to keep his pace, sometimes being led to take baby steps and at other times tremendous strides.

These steps and strides direct us to Edith's interior world, her growth in prayer, and her commitment to love. This spiritual biography, therefore, does not seek to provide a strict chronology of Edith Stein's life, although the opening chapter offers a broad overview of the most significant events. While chronological details provide a fascinating backdrop, they do not concentrate on Edith's awe-inspiring interior journey, which we will ponder. We will consider Edith's growing appreciation of the Eucharist, her deepening relationship with the Blessed Mother, and her understanding, indeed, her premonition, of the suffering she would endure. We will see her inner transformation and her growth in love of God and neighbor against the setting of two world wars.

As we consider Edith's interior life and her spiritual journey, it is helpful to keep in mind four dates:

1. October 12, 1891: Edith is born.

2. January 1, 1922: Edith is re-born, that is, baptized into the Catholic faith.

3. October 14, 1933: Edith enters religious life.

4. August 9, 1942: Edith suffers death at the hands of the Nazis.

Edith would have emphasized this last date not as an ending but as the beginning of her new life with her Creator and Redeemer. With God's help, Edith not only appreciated every stage of her earthly life, but she also looked with hope to an eternal life with him. Searching desperately for the Truth and eventually discovering a personal God who sought her friendship, Edith came to experience the warmth of God's heart drawing her into deeper intimacy. Hers was a poignant journey of seeking, discovering, and re-discovering life with God—a life Edith came to appreciate as a precious gift. As we glimpse into the mystery of that divine gift, we observe God's great blessings on an individual soul, blessings that overflowed dramatically into the lives of others. Pondering Edith's graced life, we are led to discover how Edith embraced the mission God offered to her: to carry divine life into the world.

CHAPTER 1

Carrying Divine Life into the World

E dith Stein's birthday suggested great blessings and great beginnings. She was born on the Jewish festival of Yom Kippur, the Day of Atonement. Edith's mother, Frau Auguste Stein, often reminded her daughter of the powerful significance of this day. "She laid great stress on my being born on the Day of Atonement," Edith explained, "and I believe this contributed more than anything else to her youngest's being especially dear to her."[1]

Raised in a large Jewish family in Breslau, Germany, Edith was the last of eleven children, four of whom died in infancy. Her father, Siegfried Stein, died when Edith was not yet two. An extremely sensitive child, Edith seemed to sense other people's problems, noting the pain in their faces and voices. She explained, "Whatever I saw or heard throughout my days was pondered.... The sight of a drunkard could haunt and plague me for days and nights on end."[2]

Keeping her observations to herself, she occasionally lost sleep and became ill.

> I never mentioned a word to anyone of these things which caused me so much hidden suffering. It never occurred to me that one could speak about such matters. Only infrequently did I give my family any inkling of what was happening: for no apparent reason I sometimes developed a fever and in delirium spoke of the things which were oppressing me inwardly.[3]

Her outward demeanor rarely reflected her inner turmoil. To the observer, Edith was lively, interesting, even entertaining. She read widely and could converse about a broad range of topics, including politics, poetry, literature, and history. Intelligent, precocious, and mature beyond her years, she moved easily in the world of adults as she pondered their difficulties, asked questions, and offered opinions. She could participate in weighty conversations, quoting great authors and poets and unabashedly giving her views on political issues.

By the time she was in her midteens, Edith no longer was interested in classroom learning; she decided that she "had been sitting on a school bench long enough and needed a change."[4] Part of the reason for this restlessness was a daunting new requirement of her school curriculum. She had just completed nine grades, and, up to that time, the school system had required only four more years for graduation. However, the administration changed the requirement to six years. She felt discouraged and demoralized.

She faced other disappointments, too; indeed, the first sting of discrimination occurred in grammar school. A stellar student, she consistently was at the top of her class. Yet on one occasion, she was passed over for the highest honors she clearly deserved. Edith recognized, as did many of her classmates, that she was suffering discrimination because she was Jewish. She nevertheless responded with dignified composure, and did not begrudge the other student's time in the limelight.

Edith's gift of kindness and compassion shone through in many aspects of her young life. When one of her aunts was dying of cancer, Edith and her family members accompanied the elderly woman throughout the various stages of the disease.[5] Perhaps this journey into pain and suffering prompted Edith to ponder the deeper questions that a school curriculum did not address. Some people considered her simply a daydreamer, but she actually was considering profound issues. She found that "various questions began to preoccupy [her] mind, ideological ones especially, about which there was little discussion in school."[6] Growing up physically and emotionally, Edith craved independence and asked her mother if she could leave school and go to Hamburg to stay with her sister Else and brother-in-law Max. She looked forward to helping them care for their two small children.

Frau Stein granted her daughter permission, assuring Edith: "I won't coerce you.... I allowed you to start school when you wanted to go. By the same token, you may now leave if that is what you want."[7] Elated, Edith did not hesitate: "Leaving school was anything but difficult for me. To begin with, I was fed up with learning. I did not feel close to any of my teachers."[8] She also did not feel particularly close to her classmates, most of whom she rarely saw outside of the classroom.

Edith intended to live in Hamburg for six weeks, but remained for ten months at her sister's heartfelt urging. Edith missed her family in Breslau, but did not reveal this for fear of hurting Else's feelings. Edith later realized that she was "like a chrysalis in its cocoon," isolated by miles from most of her family and family friends. "I was restricted to a very tight circle and lived in a world of my own even more exclusively than I had at home."[9] Perhaps away from home for the first time, Edith, a typical teenager, began to question her religious upbringing. Her sister Else had done the same as a young adult, forgoing the practice of any religion by the time she had married. Edith perceived that Else and Max were "utter nonbelievers."[10]

Edith went through major transformations in Hamburg. The gifted student now was "a bit apathetic intellectually."[11] She did read a lot, but not the kind of literature she had enjoyed when she was in Breslau. Even her physical appearance changed dramatically. "The slim child blossomed to almost womanly fullness; ...the blond hair of childhood darkened noticeably."[12] When she later returned to Breslau, she was mistaken for one of her cousins!

Edith also began to flounder spiritually, and she made a decision that would change the course of her young adult life. She consciously decided to stop praying. This was not a decision made lightly or impulsively. Edith would not have taken such a step without much serious deliberation. The teenager, separated from most of her family, now seemed to feel separated from God, too. She eventually would recant some decisions made during this time. She would return to school, but she would not return to her faith. The decision remained firm and unwavering throughout the rest of her teenage years and well into her twenties.

While Edith may not have divulged this choice to her family, Frau Stein seemed to have had a maternal sense of her daughter's spiritual struggles. When Edith was in her early twenties, Frau Stein expressed concern about the lack of attention Edith showed to God, and wished her daughter would be "mindful of the One to whom [she] owed this [scholarly] success."[13] Her mother cited God's hand prospering their lumber business, acknowledging its success in spite of severe obstacles, setbacks, and challenges. "After all, I can't imagine that I owe everything I've achieved to my own ability."[14]

When Edith returned to Breslau, she was ready to resume some of the activities she so enjoyed before her move. She immersed herself in reading great literature and in helping her sister Erna with her literature assignments. "At that time the thought did occur to me…actually it would be much smarter to go [back to school] myself than merely share in [Erna's] study.…"[15] However she could not return immediately, because she needed to be tutored in the subjects she had missed during her stay in Hamburg. For six months, Edith was tutored in Latin and mathematics, receiving exhaustive lessons and lengthy assignments. She worked morning through late evening. Despite the harsh schedule, Edith was delighted: "This half-year of intense work I have always remembered as the first completely happy time of my life. That may be attributable to the opportunity given me…to have my mental powers fully engaged in a task for which they were eminently suited."[16]

Finishing her tutorials, Edith returned to the classroom and immediately earned high grades and accolades. Following graduation, she enrolled at the
University of Breslau. Here she continued to wrestle
with faith questions, growing frustrated and depressed
in the process. Often she seemed to put her questions
on hold as she immersed herself in her studies, first pur-
suing child psychology and then her great love: philosophy. At the University of Breslau, she earned a reputa-
tion as a formidable scholar and, at times, an outspoken
intellectual. After four semesters at the university, she
was ready for more academic challenges. When she was
studying psychology, she read a reference to Edmund
Husserl's *Logical Investigations*. Husserl was the founder
of the phenomenological movement, and his students
and large following of admirers considered him the
"Master." He and this new branch of philosophy known
as phenomenology, the study of the essence of consciousness, fascinated Edith.

Though attracted to this philosophical approach,
Edith did not explore the topic further until a friend,
Dr. Georg Moskowitz, encouraged her to give up the
study of psychology. He urged, "Leave all that stuff aside
and just read this; after all, it's where all the others got
their ideas."[17] He handed her the second volume of
Husserl's work, and Edith spent her next vacation
devouring every page.[18] Moskowitz encouraged her to
transfer to the University of Göttingen, where she could
learn from the "Master" himself. He explained, "In
Göttingen that's all you do: philosophize day and night,
at meals, in the street, everywhere. All you talk about is
'phenomena.'"[19]

At this stage of Edith's life, it must have sounded like heaven on earth. Moskowitz's enthusiasm was contagious, and Edith excitedly considered the proposition. In typical fashion, she postponed her decision until she could give the matter serious reflection. As she pondered Moskowitz's suggestion, two seemingly unrelated events cemented Edith's decision.

First, she coincidentally saw a journal carrying a picture of Hedwig Conrad-Martius, a brilliant student of Husserl's. Moskowitz knew her, and Edith not only would come to know her professionally, but she would also become her dear friend. Many years later, in fact, Edith would ask her to be her godmother.

Second, Edith unexpectedly received an invitation to Göttingen from Nelli Neumann, recently married to Edith's cousin Richard Courant. Soon after their wedding, Nelli wrote from her new home in Göttingen to thank Frau Stein for her wedding present and to ask whether she "wouldn't...like to send Erna and Edith here to study?"[20] Edith needed no further incentives to prepare for her move. Her college friends good-naturedly teased Edith about her new path:

> Many a maiden dreams of "busserl" [kisses]
> Edith, though, of naught but Husserl.
> In Göttingen she soon will see
> Husserl as real as real can be.[21]

But not everyone was as supportive or as friendly in bidding Edith good-bye. One classmate took her to task for her critical attitude. As he said good-bye, he remarked, "Well, I wish you the good fortune of finding in Göttingen people who will satisfy your taste. Here you seem to have become far too critical."[22]

Edith was "stunned." She later pondered, "I was no longer accustomed to any form of censure. At home hardly anyone dared to criticize me; my friends showed me only affection and admiration. So I had been living in the naïve conviction that I was perfect."[23] Humbled, Edith took her friend's words to heart. She blamed her inflated view of herself on "ethical idealism," typical of those "without any faith.... Because one is enthused about what is good, one believes oneself to be good."[24] Her classmate's unexpected criticism stung her to the core, causing her to seriously ponder her own harsh judgments. She explained:

> I had always considered it my privilege to make remarks about everything I found negative, inexorably pointing out other persons' weaknesses, mistakes, or faults of which I became aware, often using a ridiculing or sarcastic tone of voice.... So these words of farewell from a man whom I esteemed and loved caused me acute distress. I was not angry with him for saying them. Nor did I shrug them off as an undeserved reproach. They were for me a first alert to which I gave much reflection.[25]

A first alert. Edith took the alarm seriously. She would watch her words and the tone she used in delivering them. She would continue to listen for other alerts— those that would slowly propel her into the world of faith. She listened to people of faith, overheard their conversations, watched their joyful expressions, and observed them in prayer. She was particularly spellbound by the lectures and life of Max Scheler, author of *Formalism in Ethics and Non-Formal Ethics of Values.* A renowned philosopher, Scheler had been banned from teaching at the university after a very public personal scandal erupted during his divorce proceedings.

Knowing that the professor could not speak on campus, the Philosophical Society, of which Edith was a member, invited him to speak at a local café. The group listened with rapt attention. Edith was impressed, even awed, by his speeches and discussions: "In no other person have I ever encountered the 'phenomenon of genius' as clearly."[26] She was equally impressed with his obvious passion at this time for Catholicism; indeed, he opened the door for Edith to reconsider faith questions. Though she did not explore the questions just yet, the seeds were planted, and they would blossom gradually throughout her university years and beyond.

Unlike her secondary school years, Edith now had a large circle of friends and acquaintances. She cultivated many close friendships, equally comfortable in the company of men or women and with people of different faith traditions. These friendships proved to be lifelong. Although Edith was not a Catholic at this time, she was aware of and appreciated the Catholic ideal of marriage. She hoped to marry someday and was interested in one young man whose name she never divulged. Roman Ingarden, a philosophy student, certainly stands out as someone of whom Edith was particularly fond, even once beginning a letter to him with the salutation, "My darling."

Another college friend, Hans Lipps, a fellow member of the Philosophical Society, "made a deeper impression on [her] than did anyone else."[27] She kept his picture on her desk and corresponded with him frequently, particularly while he served in the military during World War I. He eventually would marry, but his wife died at a young age, leaving him with two small children. When

Lipps proposed marriage to Edith soon thereafter, Edith responded that it was too late, perhaps alluding to her vocation to become a religious sister. Another college friend, Eduard Metis, obviously felt romantically interested in her. Edith, however, made it clear to him that she did not feel the same way, although she appreciated his friendship. They continued to be close friends. He died at a young age of pneumonia.

Edith also counted as friends various mentors, including the philosopher Adolf Reinach. When she had become frustrated and disillusioned in the progress of a thesis, she received valuable assistance from Dr. Reinach in his home office. She described the help he gave her in glowing terms: "I was like one reborn. All discontent with life had disappeared.... I had been rescued from distress by a good angel. By one magic word, he seemed to have transformed the monstrous offspring of my poor brain into a clear and well-organized whole."[28]

In the summer of 1914, World War I broke out and interrupted Edith's college education. When Edith heard the news of the declaration of war, she realized that her hometown of Breslau, so close to the Russian border, might be invaded. She needed to return home quickly. "Though feverishly tense, I faced the future with great clarity and determination."[29] She knew immediately that she wanted to serve as a Red Cross nurse, acknowledging, "I have no private life anymore.... All my energy must be devoted to this great happening. Only when the war is over, if I'm alive then, will I be permitted to think of my private affairs once more."[30] When she arrived home, her mother greeted her in a reassuring way. Edith later recounted the following conversation she then had with her mother:

"Don't be afraid," said my mother.

"I'm not afraid," I replied. "But it is entirely possible that the Russians will cross the border in a few days."

"Then we'll take a broomstick and beat them back."[31]

Her mother's courageous stance inspired Edith and perhaps had a contagious effect. Although the Russians did not cross the border, Edith still was not out of harm's way. In fact, she deliberately put herself at risk when she volunteered to work at a Red Cross military hospital. Despite her mother's strong objections ("granite was striking granite"), Edith resolutely left home to work at a lazaretto, a hospital for soldiers with contagious diseases.[32] When she was asked by her fellow workers why she had interrupted her studies, she replied forcefully, "All my fellow students were in the service and I could not see why I should be better off than they."[33] During her nursing career, she wore a brooch with a black bow and a red cross. She distinguished herself for her moral convictions, deep compassion, and quick grasp of languages and medicine. She also mastered lip-reading in order to help a patient who was unable to speak or write. As she assisted him in drafting a letter to his family, Edith "watched his mouth with intense concentration, read every word there, wrote it down, and then for verification showed him each phrase as [she] finished it."[34] The words were not in German but Italian!

As she continued to serve, she found herself face to face with the reality of death. For the first time in her

life, she saw patients take their dying breath. She
described in poignant words how she listened to the
breath of a desperately ill patient. "Suddenly it stopped.
I hurried to his bedside. There was no heartbeat."[35] She
followed protocol, almost perfunctorily, until she gath-
ered up his belongings. She found a small piece of
paper, given to the man by his wife, "a prayer for the
preservation of his life. Only when I saw that did I fully
realize what this death meant, humanly speaking."[36] She
did not spend much time thinking about this, but
steeled herself so that she could continue her work. "I
dared not let myself brood over that. I pulled myself
together and went to call the doctor."[37]

The more Edith realized the agony of the war, the
more she wanted to serve in a dramatic way. She wished
to serve at a hospital closer to the front and was disappointed that she was not transferred. She courageously
drew even closer to the pain of others, opening her
heart to their needs. For her courageous service, she
earned a medal of valor. By this time, her energy had
been completely sapped. She was exhausted and frail.
She had poured out her heart for others, and she suffered physically as a result.

After Edith returned home, she also experienced the
agony of personal loss. In 1917, her dear friend and
mentor, Adolf Reinach, died at the front. While Edith
mourned, she found strength and inspiration from an
unexpected source: Reinach's grieving widow, Anna.
Her Christian courage, drawn from the power of the
cross, greatly inspired Edith. The seeds of conversion
were beginning to blossom.

Others inspired Edith, too: a stranger praying in a cathedral, a friend receiving the Eucharist, a learned professor speaking in a café about philosophy and matters of faith. Edith continued her search for the truth— the great beginning of her journey to the Catholic faith. The slow and steady beginning moved into high gear when Edith happened upon the autobiography of the Carmelite mystic St. Teresa of Avila. When she read the entire book in one night, she felt catapulted from the world of question marks into one of exclamation points. "This is the Truth!" Her excited exclamation heralded a dramatic new beginning. Edith was baptized only a few months later, at the beginning of a new year: January 1, 1922.

At the start of her life as a Catholic, Edith desired to live apart from secular society, behind cloistered walls. She seemed to so identify with Teresa of Avila that she wanted immediately to join the Discalced Carmelites. She wanted to live "totally immersed in thoughts of the divine." Her spiritual director had a different beginning in mind for the new convert and the extraordinarily gifted philosopher. She should share her talents with the world; she should write, teach, and lecture. She should keep in mind her mother's reaction to her conversion. How could Frau Stein withstand her daughter's move to a convent?

Considering her spiritual director a representative of God, she took his advice seriously. She even echoed his sentiments when she later advised a new convert:

> If a religious vocation is genuine, it will endure such a
> waiting period. Should it be an illusion formed in the

first fervor, it is better to recognize this outside rather than through a serious disappointment within the monastery.[38] Edith also appreciated her spiritual director's assistance in helping her to secure a position at St. Magdalena's School for girls in Speyer. This was a training institute for teachers, run by the Dominican Sisters. Edith had been unable to obtain a university-level position because of gender discrimination, but now, with no sense of bitterness, she embraced her unexpected career of teaching and mentoring young women. She also lived with the Dominican Sisters and joined them in daily prayer. She was growing steadily in her relationship with Christ and with the countless people who continued to enter her life.

In the classroom, Edith was well respected and beloved. Challenging, yet caring, she strove to give her students a solid education in history, literature, and the German language, as well as life lessons that would benefit them long after graduation. Edith explained her goal succinctly:

> Surely the children...should gain...the strength to form their lives in the spirit of Christ. Surely it is most important that the teachers truly have this spirit themselves and vividly exemplify it. At the same time they also need to know life as the children will find it. Otherwise there will be a great danger that the girls will tell themselves: "The Sisters have no notion about the world...."[39]

Edith herself certainly was not indifferent to the secular world; rather, she was quite interested in current events and escalating crises. While she thirsted for solitary prayer, she also had a deep sense of the urgent need for self-sacrificial action *in* the world. The recognition of God's power and love in her own life led her away from any self-absorption and into selfless service. Her circle of influence widened, her level of concern intensified, and her life of prayer deepened. Edith understood that as we progress in the spiritual journey, the eternal light of God allows us to see the whole horizon; for the higher we climb, the more we are able to see the whole world. As we view the great landscape, we simultaneously see the details once obscured. We come to know the nooks and crannies, the forgotten and depressed areas, and the corners of the world that need our prayers.

This was Edith's view of the spiritual life; indeed, it reflected her own. She could see, with her heart's eye, the needs of her immediate environment as well as the larger world. The closer Edith drew to divine love, the more her eyes and her heart were opened, and the more she was ready to serve anywhere, even in dangerous circumstances. She wanted to carry divine life into the world; this was her desire and responsibility as a woman of great faith and love. She prayed and sacrificed for others, as she so vividly, even prophetically, explained in a letter of 1930, eight years after her Baptism:

> After every encounter in which I am made aware of how powerless we are to exercise direct influence, I have a deeper sense of the urgency of my own *holocaustum*.... But there can be no doubt that we are in the here-and-now to work out our salvation and that of those who have been entrusted to our souls. Let us help one another to learn more and more how to make every day and every hour part of the structure for eternity—shall we [do so] by our mutual prayers...?[40]

The eternal and the mundane: Edith could focus on both at once. How could she maintain such balance? How could she accomplish so much in her life? The sheer volume of paperwork she produced in the decade following her Baptism is amazing: essays, poems, translations, lecture notes, and even all the homework assignments she so painstakingly corrected. Still broader questions arise: After spending so much time on paperwork, how could she pick up a pen to write to a friend with a problem? How could she have done all this while finding time for prayer? How could she be so busy and yet truly present to so many people? How could she have so many deep friendships? How could she prove so reliable when her schedule taxed her so much? With all the distractions in life, how could she have been perfectly silent and still before the Lord in the tabernacle? How could she project such serenity and cheerfulness when she knew the misery in the world?

Edith—the great beginner—provided the answers: caring for others and introducing them to God's love requires not human strength but the power of God. It requires beginning the day with a focus on him. She explained this in a letter to her friend, Sister Callista Kopf:

> The only essential is that one finds, first of all, a quiet corner in which one can communicate with God as though there were nothing else, and that must be done daily. It seems to me the best time is in the early morning hours before we begin our daily work; furthermore, [it is also essential] that one accepts one's particular mission there, preferably for each day, and does not make one's own choice.

Edith continued with an instruction on the need for humility during this early morning conversation with God. "Finally," she wrote, "one is to consider oneself totally as an instrument, especially with regard to the abilities one uses to perform one's special tasks, in our case, e.g., intellectual ones. We are to see them as something used, not by us, but by God in us."[41] Only if we take our spiritual lives seriously can we take our responsibility to the world seriously. Beginning the day in God's presence enables us to reflect his presence throughout the day.

Edith learned to surrender to him daily and live at his hand. Drawing close to God in prayer and in the sacramental life of the Church, she understood that it would be impossible to carry God's life without accepting the truth that God seeks to carry us. "This security, however, is not the self-assurance of one who under her own power stands on firm ground," she explained, "but rather the sweet and blissful security of a child that is lifted up and carried by a strong arm." She continued with utter confidence:

> And when he tells me through the mouth of the prophet that he stands more faithfully at my side than my father and my mother, yea that he is love itself, then I begin to understand how "rational" is my trust in the arm that carries me and how foolish is all my fear of falling prey to nothingness—unless I tear myself loose from this sheltering hold.[42]

Edith discovered herself cradled in the love and life of God. She found herself stretched beyond the confines of her own desires and interests. The closer she was drawn by God to his life and love, the closer she became to the world. He gave her the gifts of his life and his love, and she needed to exercise good stewardship of these divine gifts. She could not keep the gifts for herself; she needed to share them, and God would help her to do so. Just as God drew her to his heart, he now was prodding her to share his heart with others.

Edith summarized her spiritual journey in a letter to a friend:

> Immediately before, and for a good while after my conversion, I was of the opinion that to lead a religious life meant one had to give up all that was secular and to live totally immersed in thoughts of the Divine. But gradually I realized that something else is asked of us in this world and that, even in the contemplative life, one may not sever the connection with the world. I even believe *that the deeper one is drawn into God*, the more one must "go out of oneself"; that is, one must go to the world in order to *carry the divine life* into it [emphases added].[43]

Written approximately six years after her Baptism, Edith's words allow us to glimpse the inner life of a woman whose public persona reflected the heights of success. Popular on the lecture circuit, she had a flourishing teaching and public speaking career and a growing list of admirers, as well as many close friendships. She knew that her intimate relationship with God was not for herself alone, but for all those with whom she came into contact.

Edith's mission of carrying divine life reflected her desire to be a vessel of divine life and an instrument of divine love. She was empowered by God's love to see his will and to do it, to understand human anguish and to seek to alleviate it. With God's grace, she would be a pillar of support to suffering humanity. She came to love greatly by experiencing the love of his Sacred Heart, by recognizing God's loving hand in all her endeavors, and by receiving his love in the sacrament of love, the Eucharist. Edith understood that truly participating in his life would mean entering deeply into the darkest nights. She would do so while continuing to radiate his divine light to a world dimmed by the shadow of sin.

Edith took up the task of spreading his word, but not as the typical missionary. In her world of academia, she entered lecture halls and gave talks in crowded auditoriums, stunning audiences with her profound knowledge of the Church and her obvious love of Christ. She amazed crowds even before she began to speak, for she carried herself with serene confidence and graceful poise. She did not seek to draw attention to herself; quite the contrary. She attracted interest and admiration simply by her humble bearing. She viewed her work as a method of evangelization, but she realized that her message might not always be well received. She knew that there would be "many a tougher battle" on behalf of Christ.[44]

Traveling throughout Germany, Austria, and Switzerland, Edith addressed such topics as "The Intrinsic Value of Women in National Life," "The Vocations of Men and Women," and "The Church, Woman, and Youth." She received great praise, although she once was criticized for being too pious. It seemed, she replied forcefully, that some "did not want the supernatural to be brought up at all. But, if I could not speak about that, I would probably not mount a lecturer's platform at all."[45]

Edith committed herself to a vocation of spreading the message of Christ wherever that might lead—even to her death. Long before the Nazis arrested her in 1942, she knew that God was calling her to embrace the cross in a radical way. While she earned accolades as a great Catholic intellectual, she kept her focus on Christ Crucified as her humility deepened and her prayer life intensified. Desiring to grow in intimacy with Christ and feeling more and more attracted to the Eucharist, Edith received Communion daily. She also came to love Mary, the maiden who truly carried Divine Life, the Christ Child, into the world, and whose maternal heart, though pierced by a sword, allowed her to stand at the foot of her Son's cross.

Edith's Eucharistic and Marian spirituality deepened as she continued her teaching career in Speyer. Despite her close relationship with the Sisters, Edith never entertained the idea of becoming a Dominican nun. She did, however, consider this a time of spiritual beginnings—a preparation for becoming a Carmelite nun. She continued to discern this calling to the religious life even after she left her residence in the Dominican convent and returned to her mother's home. There she was able to spend solitary time studying and translating St. Thomas Aquinas without the interruptions of academic life. Within months, though, she returned to the classroom, this time at the Catholic Pedagogical Institute in Münster. Although the new job brought her much excitement and fulfillment, it would not last long, for the political situation was threatening her livelihood, as well as her very life.

The world was becoming more chaotic and terror-filled; it was in urgent need of prayer and sacrifice. To this society, even to Nazis in Gestapo offices near the end of her life, Edith spoke the truth of Christ: "Praised be Jesus Christ!"[46] With a sense of urgency, Edith recognized the responsibility of people of faith to illuminate the dark "night of sin." She urged, "The more an era is engulfed in the night of sin and estrangement from God the more it needs souls united to God. And God does not permit a deficiency. The greatest figures of prophecy and sanctity step forth out of the darkest night."[47]

In April 1933, only months after she began to teach in Münster, Edith's teaching career came to an abrupt end. She realized that anti-Semitism had effectively closed the door to her teaching career at the institute, and it would not be long before she was banned from teaching anywhere in Germany. She took the news calmly, for she recognized that the door to the Carmelite convent might now open for her. With her spiritual director's permission, Edith applied to enter the Carmelite monastery—her dream for more than a decade. The community accepted her warmly, and she was able to move to the Carmelite monastery in Cologne six months later.

Before entering Carmel, Edith had taken up the challenge and mission to give the light and love of God. She continued to accept this challenge and mission as she entered a cloistered convent as Sister Teresa Benedicta of the Cross. A change of location and name did not change her commitment to the world. Her religious name testified to her commitment to live the Christian life wholeheartedly; she truly carried the cross as her title and in the very depths of her soul.

Edith never took her religious life for granted. She treasured the grace of her vocation and appreciated each renewal of vows as an opportunity to begin again. She knew that when she and her fellow Sisters faithfully responded to their vocations, Christ gave them, in a special way, the gift of his divine life. The gift, however, was "not a one-time event."[48] She believed that God desired that the Carmelites deliberately renew their search for him. As St. Augustine explained, "God lets himself be sought...to let himself be found. He lets himself be found to be sought again." Edith understood that the renewal of vows responded to this need to begin again. She realized:

> After each great hour of grace, it is as if we were but beginning now to understand our vocation. Therefore an interior need prompts us to renew our vows repeatedly. To each...renewal of vows, the divine Child responds with renewed acceptance and a deeper union. And this means a new, hidden operation of grace in our souls.[49]

God's grace would sustain the seeker through many new beginnings, and the search would continue to intensify as the relationship mysteriously deepened.

Edith believed that the nuns' faithful commitment to their religious vows grew all the more crucial as "overwhelming misery" threatened society. In 1934, one year after Adolf Hitler came to power and Edith joined Carmel, she wrote, "In our time, when the powerlessness of all natural means for battling the overwhelming misery everywhere has been demonstrated so obviously, an entirely new understanding of the power of prayer, of expiation, and of vicarious atonement has again awakened."[50] Referring to St. Teresa of Avila, her namesake, she urged, "One would like to bring into our times...something of the spirit of this great woman who built amazingly during a century of battles and disturbances."[51] Edith herself would build "amazingly"— building bridges to the suffering world through her prayers and sacrifices. She knew all the more that "one may not sever the connection with the world."[52] Far from it; she cemented this connection from behind the cloistered walls.

To her college friend Fritz Kaufmann she hinted that her life of prayer was a way to grow closer to those outside the convent. "I have other ways and means of keeping the bonds alive," she explained.[53] To the poet and novelist Gertrud von le Fort, Edith assured, "You must not believe that you will lose anything at all. Everyone who has a place in my heart and in my prayers can only gain."[54]

From her convent room, Edith wrote many letters that testify to her great love of family and friends. These letters overflow with encouragement and compassion. She also wrote many inspirational essays and fictional dialogues, and the closer she came to her own martyrdom, the more heartfelt her writings became. Indeed, even the opening lines of one of her poems bear witness to Edith Stein, the great writer, the great beginner. The poem, "And I Remain with You: From a Pentecost Novena," begins with these compelling lines:

Who are you, sweet light, that fills me
And illumines the darkness of my heart? You lead me
like a mother's hand,

And should you let go of me,
I would not know how to take another step....
Are you not the sweet manna
That from the Son's heart
Overflows into my heart,
The food of angels and the blessed?...
And he gives me new life from day to day,
And at some time his fullness is to stream through me,
Life of your life—indeed, you yourself:
Holy Spirit—eternal life! [55]

Edith relied all the more on the Holy Spirit to guide her steps, to teach her what was needed to carry divine life into a world at war. As the war intensified, and her own death drew nearer, she trusted in the Holy Spirit's power to enlighten the darkened world. In 1940, two years before her death, Edith wrote an essay, "The Hidden Life and Epiphany," with opening words that reflect the hope that God's light will shine in a darkened world: "When the gentle light of the advent candles begins to shine in the dark days of December—a mysterious light in a mysterious darkness—it awakens in us the consoling thought that the divine light, the Holy Spirit, has never ceased to illumine the darkness of the fallen world." [56]

She wrote these words after Kristallnacht, the "night of broken glass," when the Nazis pillaged and destroyed Jewish homes, businesses, and synagogues. Edith continued to ponder the nightmarish events of November 9 and 10, 1936, even after she was transferred to the apparent safety of Echt, Holland. Edith did not feel secure there, but she calmly focused on her eternal home. It would not be long before the Nazis invaded Holland. Although they jeopardized Edith's life, she

focused not on herself but on her family, friends—
indeed, the whole suffering world.

Edith begged her Carmelite Sisters to understand the
power of their vows to extinguish the flames of the
chaotic world. She pleaded:

> The world is in flames. Are you impelled to put them
> out? Look at the cross. From the open heart gushes the
> blood of the Savior. This extinguishes the flames of hell.
> Make your heart free by the faithful fulfillment of your
> vows; then the flood of divine love will be poured into
> your heart until it overflows and becomes fruitful to all
> the ends of the earth.[57]

Having volunteered during the First World War,
Edith identified well with the Sisters' desire to heal the
wounded world. She understood that the cloistered
Sisters wanted to help, as she did, in a tangible way. She
asked:

> Do you hear the groans of the wounded on the
> battlefields in the west and the east? You are not a physi-
> cian and not a nurse and cannot bind up the wounds.
> You are enclosed in a cell and cannot get to them. Do
> you hear the anguish of the dying? You would like to be
> a priest and comfort them. Does the lament of the wid-
> ows and orphans distress you? You would like to be an
> angel of mercy and help them.[58]

Edith knew that she and all the Sisters could make a
difference by faithful prayer and sacrifice, indeed by
their very being. She encouraged the Sisters:

> Look at the Crucified. If you are nuptially bound to him
> by the faithful observance of your holy vows, your *being*
> is precious blood. Bound to him, you are omnipresent
> as he is. You cannot help here or there like the physi-
> cian, the nurse, the priest. You can be at all fronts, wher-

ever there is grief, in the power of the cross. Your compassionate love takes you everywhere, this love from the divine heart. Its precious blood is poured everywhere— soothing, healing, saving.[59]

Edith's compassionate love accompanied her on many travels throughout her life, even on her final train ride to the gas chamber of Auschwitz in August 1942. When the Nazis arrested her after the Dutch bishops spoke out against Nazism, Edith remained prayerful and calm. Thinking that they were sending her to a work camp, Edith responded with characteristic optimism: she would begin anew. *"So far I prayed and worked, from now on I will work and pray."*[60]

Even as she headed to her death, she remained committed to introducing others to the life and love of God. She impressed inmates and guards by her kindness and serenity. Two people who brought provisions to the camps attested: "Sister Benedicta was glad she was able to help with comforting words and prayers. Her deep faith created about her an atmosphere of heavenly life."[61] Twenty years after her Baptism, Edith entered a camp where dark terror reigned. But even in that corner of the world, an evil place designed for death, her mission to carry divine life into the world still shone brightly.

CHAPTER 2

Searching for the Truth: Edith Stein's Spiritual Quest

Edith's childhood began with a prediction of great-ness—one that she herself made. She was convinced she would have a great future, though she did not know how that greatness would unfold or what form it would take. This optimism stayed with her as she journeyed into her teens, even as she surrendered the one anchor that could strengthen her steps and enlighten her journey—the anchor of prayer. In her midteens, she "gave up praying.... I took no thought of my future although I continued to live with the conviction that I was destined for something great."[1]

Throughout the rest of her teenage years and most of her twenties, Edith did not embrace religious matters. After returning from Hamburg, she had a lot of spare time, and she threw herself into reading, loving every minute of this solitary endeavor. Shakespeare became her "daily bread."[2] Following the example of her sister Erna, she now desired to go back to the classroom. In preparation for that return, she needed extensive tutoring, an opportunity she relished. It was as though her intellectual life had been put on hold and suddenly had taken off at full speed. Easily losing herself in her books, she became "totally oblivious of all the world outside...."[3] She was particularly fond of Latin, considering it fascinating, even entertaining. "It was as though I were learning my mother tongue. That it was the language of the Church and that later I should pray in this language never even occurred to me at the time."[4]

After finishing her tutorials and passing her exams, Edith returned to formal schooling. Questions about her future became the focus of family gatherings. What should Edith do with her life?

Enthusiastic and insistent input came from her mother and siblings, as well as extended family members. They suggested such varied fields as photography, art, journalism, and medicine. Her mother suggested law, a fascinating proposition considering that women were not permitted to pursue the legal profession in Germany at that time.[5] Frau Stein gave Edith "full freedom of choice" in her decision and seemed perturbed by how family members were forcefully weighing in on the topic. She assured Edith: "No one has a right to tell you what to do. After all, no one's making us a contribution toward it. Do whatever you think is right for you."[6] The range of possibilities revealed the depth and breadth of Edith's interests and abilities. Edith rejected all these ideas and decided to pursue philosophy, a choice that seemed, in the disapproving opinion of many of her relatives, to "give no thought at all to the practical side of life!"[7]

Even as she focused on her education, Edith was attuned to her surroundings and to the problems and struggles of friends and relatives. When Edith was nineteen, her cousin Walter died, and Edith was particularly sensitive to the grief of his young Christian widow. During the funeral, Edith noticed that the widow was "inconsolable.... When the rabbi had said the final prayers and the whole group of mourners turned to leave, the young woman knelt down at the grave and, in her grief, prayed the Lord's Prayer aloud." Edith found herself touched by the expression of faith. "Naturally, that was something totally unheard-of in a Jewish cemetery but, instead of being offended by it, all were deeply moved."[8]

This would not be the last time Edith was moved by seeing a woman in prayer or by the grief of a Christian widow. In a few years, Edith would be profoundly impressed by observing two women of faith—one a grieving widow, and the other a complete stranger. Still years away from returning to prayer, she did, indeed, mourn, but not the same mourning experienced by her cousin's widow. Rather, her grief was for the state of the world. She felt saddened and helpless in the face of societal ills, frivolous pursuits, and superficial living.

She experienced a period of depression that was triggered, at least in part, by reading the popular novel *Helmut Harringa*. Horrified at its portrayal of student life as one of alcohol abuse, wild parties, and immoral behavior, Edith, now twenty-one, found no joy in life, and she began to distance herself from her friends. Her depression eventually began to lift when she attended a Bach concert at which she heard the hymn, "A Mighty

Fortress Is Our God." Inspired by the theme of truth conquering evil, Edith instantly realized that "the world might be evil; but if the small group of friends in whom I had confidence and I strove with all our might, we should certainly have done with all 'devils.'"[9]

Clearly, Edith was sensitive to the reality of the evil in the world and appreciated friendship's role in overcoming that evil. She also was convinced of the victory of truth. Although she was still without faith, she later would say that searching for truth was a prayer in itself.

At this time, Edith would emphasize human power. Her group of friends would strive with all their might to conquer "all devils." She did not rely on God; indeed, she still did not believe. As a student of philosophy, she remained apart from the world of faith, even as she became friends with many Christian converts who showed great enthusiasm for their religion.

> Persons with whom I associated daily, whom I esteemed and admired, lived in it. At the least, they deserved my giving it some serious reflection. For the time being, I did not embark on a systematic investigation of the questions of faith; I was far too busy with other matters.[10]

Busy with philosophical work, Edith sought to quench her thirst for knowledge, but she mostly ignored another search—the spiritual longing that seemed, at times, to disturb and even haunt her. Many years would pass before she would understand that "The way of faith gives us more than the way of philosophic knowledge. Faith reveals to us the God of personal nearness, the loving and merciful God...."[11]

Most of the questions that plagued her mind and heart remained unarticulated, but she once broke the silence to ask a friend if he believed in a personal God. When he replied, "God is spirit; nothing more could be said on the subject," she felt as though she "had been handed a stone instead of bread."[12]

As she continued to experience spiritual confusion and emptiness, Edith became friendly with a number of Catholic converts who attended daily Mass. She respected the faith she herself lacked. When a fellow student asked her if she belonged to this group going to daily Mass, she replied with a simple "No." She later confessed that she had wanted to add, "unfortunately."[13]

Edith kept her struggle a secret. Even as she considered the theme of "connectedness" for her doctoral dissertation on empathy, she embarked on a solitary path of searching for the truth, at times working herself into "a state of veritable despair."[14] Her university years continued to be plagued by restlessness and frustration, yet her friendships multiplied and deepened as she spent time hiking, sightseeing, and conversing about literature and current events. She also engaged in scholarly and lively conversations about philosophy, joining fellow students in the Philosophical Society.

In her early twenties, Edith listened with rapt attention to the well-prepared and powerfully delivered lectures of the philosopher Max Scheler.[15] Finding him "ingenious," "dazzling," and "handsome," Edith was captivated by his every word.[16] She was particularly inspired by Scheler's talks on faith and holiness, although his words did not serve immediately as catalysts for conversion. Edith admitted, however, that the lectures shook the "barriers of rationalistic prejudices" as she encountered "the world of faith."[17]

Scheler's influence, Edith said, "affected me...far beyond the sphere of philosophy...he was quite full of Catholic ideas at the time and employed all the brilliance of his spirit and his eloquence to plead them."[18] Awestruck yet unconvinced, Edith continued to search for the truth and "almost without noticing it, became gradually transformed."[19] More than a decade later, she realized that great beginnings in the spiritual journey do not necessarily begin with trumpet blasts, but with soft whispers, not "chisel blows" but "quiet finger stroke[s]."[20] Scheler's lectures were like those soft whispers and gentle strokes, serenely leading her to embrace the Christian faith.

Scheler was not the only philosopher who inspired Edith's gradual transformation. Adolf Reinach and his wife, Anna, both converts to Lutheranism, played pivotal roles in Edith's conversion. During Christmastime, 1915, while the First World War was raging, Reinach returned home for a short leave from his military service. Edith, now twenty-four years old, was invited to spend some time with the couple and their family and close friends. Like Reinach, Edith had spent many months away from Göttingen serving the war effort. Reinach had impressed Edith at the very start of the war with his immediate resolve to fight for his country. When one student asked him, "Must you go, also, Doctor?" he replied, "It's not that I *must*; rather, I'm permitted to go."[21] Edith had not anticipated seeing Reinach until the end of the war, so she was delighted at the opportunity to reconnect with him and with many of her other college friends.

Arriving in Göttingen a few days before Christmas, Edith enjoyed meeting old friends and acquaintances. On Christmas Eve, one friend invited Edith to attend midnight Mass, and Edith readily agreed. She recalled in detail that trip to the Catholic Church:

> So we went to the Kurze Strasse that dark winter night. But there was not a soul in sight anywhere, and when we arrived at the church we found the door securely locked. Apparently the Mass of Christmas was to be celebrated only in the morning. Disappointed, we had to go home.[22]

Did Edith feel again as though she had received a stone rather than bread?

On Christmas Day, she and many of her philosopher friends, including the Reinachs, enjoyed a festive gathering at the home of Edmund Husserl and his wife, Malvine. Edith appreciated the jovial reunion, though she did not embrace the religious significance of this holy day.[23] She joined in conversation about philosophy and even the origin of the Christmas tree.

In subsequent months, Edith took a break from her doctoral studies and visited Frankfurt, where she walked through the old part of the city with Reinach's sister, Pauline Reinach. During their walk, they decided to enter the imposing Frankfurt Cathedral. They stepped into the cathedral just for a few minutes—a brief time that would leave an indelible memory:

> ... [W]hile we looked around in respectful silence, a woman carrying a market basket came in and knelt down in one of the pews to pray briefly. This was something entirely new to me. To the synagogues or to the Protestant churches which I had visited, one went only for services.[24]

The incident awakened Edith's natural curiosity:

... [H]ere was someone interrupting her everyday shopping errands to come into this church, although no other person was in it, as though she were here for an intimate conversation. I could never forget that.[25]

The stranger surely had been carrying more than a market basket; she carried her faith and the witness of her prayer life. Although the two women never spoke, the incident introduced Edith to the life of faith and to friendship with God himself. The woman did not need to say a word to be inspiring, for her silent prayer conveyed a mysterious, hidden relationship with God. Edith would carry the sight of this stranger with her throughout her life. The experience seemed to foreshadow what would become Edith's own understanding of prayer: an intimate conversation with God. It foreshadowed, too, Edith's role in inspiring others as she knelt for hours before the Blessed Sacrament.

Edith's trip to Frankfurt also included a visit to the Liebig Museum, where she again found herself awestruck. Pausing silently before a sculpture of the Mother of God and John, along with Mary Magdalene and Nicodemus, Edith found it difficult to move on, for the sight had "an overpowering effect" on her.[26] She never elaborated on the particulars of that experience, but clearly Edith's day away from her studies enriched her spiritually. On that day, she also saw the Castle of Heidelberg and other famous sites, but "something ...made a deeper impression" on her—a church with a dividing wall down its center so that Protestants and Catholics could worship under the same roof.[27]

With these spiritual images planted deep within her, Edith returned to her studies. For the young philosopher seeking the truth and growing more spiritually restless each year, the world of faith seemed to be drawing near, and becoming a part of her life, even without her specific assent. For now, she simply would ponder. She pondered why the woman with a market basket would seem to be talking with someone in the cathedral, though "no one" was present. She pondered why her newly baptized friends radiated happiness; she envied their daily reception of the Eucharist. Indeed, the Eucharistic Lord seemed to be drawing Edith to him like a magnet.

Perhaps Edith saw a transformation in the new converts who attended daily Mass. Perhaps she noticed a sense of peace in her friends and the prayerful woman. Perhaps it was their joy. Perhaps, above all, Edith sensed their intimacy with God. Hunger for an intimate relationship with God: perhaps this is the key to understanding Edith's spiritual journey. Indeed, she expressed as much when she asked her friend about the existence of a personal God. Edith was looking for a relationship such as her friends and the stranger seemed to have with God. Could it be that Edith sensed their lives were shaped by a relationship with the Eucharistic Lord? Did she begin to re-examine her teenage decision to stop praying? Did her search for the truth intensify?

For the time being, Edith would immerse herself in her doctoral studies, earning her degree summa cum laude in 1916. She still lacked faith, but not for long. The following year would prove to be spiritually momentous for the young philosopher.

In January, Edith noticed how Adolf Reinach seemed to have deepened his religious outlook as he continued his military service. Edith's own service had not had the same spiritual impact. As she drew close to the suffering soldiers, Edith seemed to journey no closer to God. Reinach, on the other hand, "discovered, at the front, that he has no talent for philosophy... [and was] totally engrossed in religious questions...."[28] Only a few months after this religious awakening, Reinach died on the battlefield.

The loss of her friend overwhelmed Edith, and she knew that Reinach's widow, Anna, must be grieving even more. When Anna invited Edith to her home to sort out Adolf's philosophical papers, Edith hesitated, but ultimately obliged. Crossing the threshold of that home would become not only a gesture of friendship, but also a significant step toward faith in Jesus Christ. Immediately, Edith was struck by Anna's courage, her ability to stand tall in the midst of grief. Here was a woman who, in her own way, carried divine life as she carried the cross of Christ. Edith's encounter with such living faith signified a new beginning, an encounter with the great destiny she once predicted. Through Anna, Edith was introduced to the living person of Christ.

Perhaps Edith now could apply her praise of Reinach to his wife: "I felt as though I had been rescued from distress by a good angel."[29] Edith had once said that Reinach had helped her so much in her progress in philosophical studies that she had felt "reborn." Now, she was experiencing more than an intellectual rebirth; she stood on the threshold of a spiritual epiphany.

The world of Christian faith suddenly overpowered her:

> This was my first encounter with the cross and the divine strength that it inspires in those who bear it. For the first time I saw before my very eyes the Church, born of Christ's redemptive suffering, victorious over the sting of death. It was the moment in which my unbelief was shattered, Judaism paled, and Christ radiated before me: Christ in the mystery of the cross.[30]

Just as the woman kneeling in a quiet, seemingly empty church inspired Edith, now Anna Reinach, a woman who stood strong in her time of grief, inspired the young philosopher. In an instant, Edith discovered the power of the cross. As years passed, that surprise discovery would grow into a firm conviction. Edith seemed to have become one of the people she had described in her doctoral dissertation when she wrote: "There have been people who thought that in a sudden change of their person they experienced the effect of the grace of God...."[31] Now Edith found herself changed, and she knew that the grace of God had changed her. She would never be the same.

Although Edith's "unbelief shattered" in 1917, she did not embrace Catholicism until 1921. During the intervening years, she still seemed to experience a spiritual uncertainty, and she turned her attention to religious books, including the *Spiritual Exercises* of St. Ignatius. She stumbled upon the *Exercises* in a bookstore, and soon found herself not only reading the book, but also making a thirty-day Ignatian retreat on her own.[32] At the time, she probably told no one of her interest in

Catholicism or her prayer experience. The *Exercises* seemed to prepare Edith for another book she would later discover: The *Autobiography of Teresa of Avila*.

Before finding the autobiography in a friend's library, Edith continued to give much studious attention to philosophical works. She pursued her passion for philosophy with relentless energy, but not without setbacks. Despite graduating with highest honors, she could not obtain a teaching position at the university level because she was a woman. For approximately two years after graduation, she worked as an assistant to her mentor, Edmund Husserl, organizing and editing volumes of his philosophical writings.

Because she did not secure a permanent position at a university, Edith returned to her mother's house, where the parlor was converted into Edith's office. There, Edith engaged in scholarly research and writing. Inwardly and secretively, an intense trial assailed her. "I was passing through a personal crisis," she explained, "which was totally concealed from my relatives, one I was unable to resolve in our house."[33]

Though she did not express her spiritual journey in words to her family, she did give them a major clue in the form of a portrait. Above Edith's desk hung a picture of St. Francis of Assisi by Cimabue, the thirteenth-century Italian artist who portrayed Francis with the stigmata.[34] Could Edith have prayed for the intercession of St. Francis as she struggled with questions of faith?

That picture of St. Francis hung in the parlor when Edith's sister Erna, now a medical doctor, was married there in the winter of 1920. This filled Edith with consolation and inspiration. "At that time my health was very poor, probably as a result of the spiritual conflicts I then endured in complete secrecy and without any human support."[35] Her suffering was so acute "that the slightest sound made me cringe....[Erna] said she could not stand it any more, and gave me a small dose of morphine."[36]

Edith enjoyed the wedding, and when the day ended she made a firm resolution to take care of herself. It was time to discern her religious identity and vocation. Before she said good-bye to her sister and brother-in-law, she gave them a wedding present, a poem she had written for the occasion. It demonstrates her creativity and humor, but perhaps it also foreshadows her own transition to a new life. In the poem, a stork encounters babies who have yet to be conceived and says:

> Here you simply cannot stay.
> This Camp ain't forever, no, it's not,
> From here you must go to another spot...
> Look through my spyglass, and don't tarry.
> You'll see a couple who just did marry...[37]

If Edith could have looked through a "spyglass" on the day of her sister's wedding, she would have seen that she, herself, was going "to another spot." In a few short months she would experience a spiritual epiphany.

Beginning of a New Life with Christ

In the summer of 1921, Edith visited her friend Hedwig Conrad-Martius, a fellow philosopher and a student of Husserl's. Conrad-Martius had recently converted to Lutheranism and she had a well-stocked library of Christian books. Alone in her library one night, Edith happened upon the *Autobiography of St. Teresa of Avila*, a title she may have heard of in Husserl's lectures.[38] She read the entire book quickly, devouring it as if she urgently needed nourishment. Finishing the last page, Edith excitedly realized, "This is the Truth!" Perhaps in Teresa she saw a strong woman of faith and courage similar to Anna Reinach, who had introduced Edith to the mystery of the cross. Now Teresa introduced her to the whole mystery of a lived relationship with Christ, the Way, the Truth, and the Life. Immediately, Edith bought a prayer book and a catechism. After studying both, she met a parish priest and asked to be baptized. He hesitated but quizzed her (as she requested), and was duly impressed.

January 1922 signaled not only the beginning of a new year for Edith, but of a new life with Christ. Joyfully receiving Baptism on January 1, and first Holy Communion the following day, Edith seemed to exemplify words she later wrote about a Carmelite Sister's youthful reception of Communion: "She was like the deer that has found water, like a child in the arms of its mother."[39]

The years of wandering and searching had come to an end; now a blissful sense of security enveloped her. Years later, from the depths of her experience, Edith advised a young friend preparing for Baptism about her own journey to the sacraments and the way that had led her to such inner contentment. She explained:

> One should be able to prepare oneself in peace. I was lucky in that way. It is in the nature of such an event that before the decisive step is taken, you see before you once more all you will be renouncing and risking. That

is how it ought to be...you place yourself totally in God's hands, then all the deeper and more beautiful will be the security attained.[40]

In many ways, Edith now personified her description of the wise men before the Incarnate Truth:

> Because God is Truth and because he wants to be found by those who seek him with their whole hearts, sooner or later the star had to appear to show these *wise men* the way to truth. And so they now stand before the Incarnate Truth, bow down and worship it....[41]

Edith was shown the way to truth—Incarnate Truth, Jesus Christ himself—and would spend the rest of her life worshipping God by prayer, sacrifice, and a life of committed love.

Years after her Baptism, Edith wrote a fictional dialogue between St. Augustine and St. Ambrose. In it, Augustine's words sound so similar to Edith's difficult journey to the Christian faith: "I sought truth.... My spirit brooded in unrest." Edith also conveyed Ambrose's appreciation of Monica's tears shed for her son's conversion: "...she now weeps sweet tears of joy, And she is richly rewarded for all her suffering."[42]

Edith's own mother was weeping over Edith's conversion, but not "sweet tears of joy". A few friends and family members were confused and hurt by her decision, but none as strongly as Frau Stein. Edith described the situation to her friend, Gertrud von le Fort, explaining that her mother

> ...declines anything that is beyond her Jewish faith. For that reason, too, it was impossible at this time to say anything to her that might have somewhat explained the step I have taken. She particularly rejects conversions.

Everyone ought to live and die in the faith in which they were born.[43]

To be the cause of her mother suffering so much pain was a difficult cross for Edith to bear. It broke Edith's heart to break her mother's heart. Considering her mother's heart-wrenching reaction to her conversion, Edith took great care not to inflict a second blow; she put aside, for the time being, her wish to enter a cloistered Carmelite convent.[44] Her spiritual director, Father Joseph Schwind, vicar general of the Diocese of Speyer, shared her concern for Frau Stein. He encouraged Edith to pursue her teaching career instead of entering Carmel, convinced that her many scholarly talents could benefit the Church and society.

Although Edith found Father Schwind's guidance difficult to hear and all the more difficult to follow, she listened respectfully and did not take any steps toward Carmel. She came to appreciate his role as her spiritual director, as well as a father figure and friend who inspired her with "his pure love of God."[45] As she later shared with a friend, she learned that one's vocation "cannot be solved merely through self-examination plus a scrutiny of the available possibilities. One must pray for the answer... and, in many cases, it must be sought by way of obedience."[46]

Edith took seriously Father Schwind's advice and realized the wisdom of his words, particularly when she met with her mother for the first time after receiving the sacraments. She was certain that Frau Stein

would not be able to withstand this second blow for the time being. She would not die of it, but it would fill her with such bitterness that I could not take the responsibility for that. I would have to wait patiently. My spiritual counselors assured me of this over and over.[47]

Although the waiting period would be longer than she anticipated, as the years passed, Edith realized that "one may not set a deadline for the Lord."[48] Her own advice to a new convert makes it clear that Edith was at peace with the delay:

> For the moment I would say: remain patiently at your job as long as you do not receive a definite hint from above to undertake something else. Use your free time to get to know and to love God and the Church better: the doctrines of the faith, the liturgy, our saints; but also the religious institutions and Catholic life in the present time, along with its shadows, which will not remain concealed from you in the long run.[49]

This was the way Edith spent the beginning of her life as a Catholic; she immersed herself in the Catholic faith, studying Church history, reading Scripture and the lives of the saints, participating in daily Mass, and praying daily for long periods of time. She came to understand:

> God leads each of us on an individual way; one reaches the goal more easily and more quickly than another. We can do very little ourselves, compared to what is done to us. But that little bit we must do. Primarily, this consists before all else of persevering in prayer to find the right way, and of following without resistance the attraction of grace when we feel it. Whoever acts in this way and perseveres patiently will not be able to say that his efforts were in vain.[50]

Consistent with these words, Edith continued to persevere patiently as she humbly submitted to God's plan. She seemed to be living out her words to a friend:

... [L]ay all care for the future, confidently, in God's hands, and allow yourself to be led by him entirely, as a child would. Then you can be sure not to lose your way. Just as the Lord brought you into his church, so he will lead you to the place in it that he wants you to have.[51]

Living the Catholic Faith in the World

Having grown in humility, Edith was able to encourage others to surrender their self-will and to allow God to direct their life's journey. Edith urged an old friend who was struggling with faith and his path in life:

Become like a child and lay your life *with* all the searching and ruminating into the Father's hand. If that cannot yet be achieved, then plead; plead with the unknown and doubted God for help in reaching it. Now you look at me in amazement that I do not hesitate to come to you with wisdom as simple as that of a child. It *is* wisdom *because* it is simple, and all mysteries are concealed in it. And it is a way that most certainly leads to the goal.[52]

With such humble surrender, Edith embarked on her new life as a Catholic, ready for new paths and adventures, including a new teaching career and a new home. With Father Schwind's help, she obtained a teaching position at an all-girls school, St. Magdalena's, in Speyer, and found a place to live at the Dominican convent attached to the school. Keeping to the nuns' schedule, she rose early every morning to pray alone, and then joined the Sisters for community prayer and Mass.

During these teaching years, Edith confessed to "living behind the sheltering walls of a convent, at heart... like a real nun, even though I wear no veil and am not bound by vows or enclosure."[53] Considering the Dominican convent a prelude to Carmel, Edith savored the time of preparation while looking forward to the day when her spiritual director would permit her to apply to enter the Carmelites.

In addition to praying, researching, and teaching, Edith was busy translating the letters of John Henry Cardinal Newman from English into German, and St. Thomas' *Disputed Questions on Truth* from Latin into German. While she embarked on this tedious task, she made a discovery that would help her to be at peace about time spent away from formal prayer. She realized that her time outside of Church, even her academic work, could glorify God. She explained to a colleague: "That it is possible to worship God by doing scholarly research is something I learned, actually, only when I was busy with [translating].... Only thereafter could I decide to resume serious scholarly research."[54]

Edith's faith was an integral part of her identity, touching and making its mark on everything she undertook. She knew, as she once advised:

> Religion is not something to be relegated to a quiet corner or for a few festive hours, but rather, as you yourself perceive, it must be the root and basis of all life: and that, not merely for a few chosen ones, but for every true Christian....[55]

In the little spare time Edith had, she engaged in lively conversation with her students, listening to their problems and their dreams, and encouraging them on their unique journeys. She strove to give her students a moral foundation so that they could enter the "real world" grounded in Christian virtue.

One of Edith's pupils later remembered:

> With very few words—just by her personality and everything that emanated from her—she set me on my way, not only in my studies, but in my whole moral life. With her you felt that you were in an atmosphere of everything noble, pure, and sublime that simply carried you up with it.[56]

She impressed not only her young students, but also her larger audiences of notable scholars, priests, religious, and lay men and women who packed lecture halls to hear Dr. Stein's wisdom. Within only six years of her conversion, Edith had become a popular speaker on the topic of Christian spirituality, particularly on the vocation of women. Her lecturing career hit her "like an avalanche."[57] Almost overnight, she became esteemed as an expert on matters of faith. One of her first talks, "Ethos of Women's Professions," received such high acclaim that she was showered with many more invitations to speak to various Catholic audiences. She was highly praised for the substance of her talks, as well as the manner of her delivery. She appeared confident yet humble. Perhaps the audience detected Edith's authenticity, the consistency between her words and her actions. She could speak of humility because she was humble; she could speak of the importance of doing God's will because she strove daily to know and follow his will.

At a time when Edith was earning rave reviews for her inspiring lectures and good works, she responded faithfully to God's call to be self-forgetful and self-giving. She had come a long way from the young student who was chastised for thinking too highly of herself and for being too proud of her talents and accomplishments. She had grown from the young woman who dismissed her mother's advice to one who remembered God's hand in life's successes. She humbly acknowledged God's presence and power in her life and work.

Occasionally, some people criticized Edith's lectures. One of her freinds took exception to how pious her talks seemed. Edith's response was unequivocal. She would continue her public speaking with the same emphasis: *"How to go about living at the Lord's hand."*[58]

Another friend noted that all the attention and praise that Edith received caused her to "become" someone—a comment that Edith strongly disavowed: "...I cannot agree.... It does appear as though the orbit of my daily duties is to expand. But that, in my opinion, does not change anything about me. It has been demanded of me, and I have undertaken it...."[59]

Many demands continued to encroach on Edith's time, including requests from numerous friends and strangers seeking her counsel. One of the Dominican Sisters remembered:

> God alone can know to how many people she gave her help, advice and direction, how often she came as an angel of charity to the relief of spiritual and bodily need. The pressure on her was often great.[60]

Edith did not succumb to the pressure; indeed, she continued to project a sense of dignified tranquillity. She explained, "...I have to budget my time so carefully.... Many people come to me and everyone who comes, hoping to find some help from me, is heartily welcome."[61]

At the same time, she had no illusions that she alone could solve everyone's problems:

I am only a tool of the Lord. I would like to lead to him anyone who comes to me. And when I notice that this is not the case, but that the interest is invested in my person, then I cannot serve as a tool and must beg the Lord to help in other ways. After all, he is never dependent on only one individual.[62]

Helping to lead others to the Catholic faith, Edith recognized that she was never the primary reason for their conversion, just the *causa secunda*, that is, the secondary cause. With deep humility, Edith considered it a joy and a privilege to collaborate with God. She realized that God's

greatest creative joy...is
That under his hand the image stirs,...
The life that he himself has placed in it
And that now answers him from within
To chisel blows or gentle finger stroke.

Beautifully capturing the privilege of collaborating with God in his work on an individual soul, Edith poetically wrote:

...often a person does not hear
The soft voice that speaks within.
Perhaps she hears the soft beating of the wings
Of the dove, but does not understand where its flight
Is drawing her. Then someone else must come,
Gifted with a finer ear attuned and keener sight,
And disclose the meaning of the obscure words.
This is the guide's wonderful gift,
The highest that, according to a sage's word,
The Creator has given to the creation:
To be his fellow worker in the salvation of souls.[63]

These fellow workers, Edith noted in an essay on spirituality, are needed in a society thirsting for God, to be used "as instruments to awaken and nurture the divine spark." [64]

Those who allow God's hands to shape and nurture their lives "exert a mysterious magnetic appeal on thirsty souls." She explained that

> streams of living water flow from all those who live in God's hand.... Without aspiring to it, they must become guides of other persons striving to the light; they must practice spiritual maternity, begetting and drawing sons and daughters nearer to the kingdom of God. The history of the Church reveals that many persons...went this way "in the world."[65]

As Edith continued her path "in the world," that is, outside religious life, she regularly received spiritual direction from Father Schwind; he encouraged her in her prayer life and in her spiritual reading, recommending books and later discussing them with her. He introduced her to his family and invited Edith to family gatherings. With Father Schwind's help, Edith delved deeply into Catholicism and learned how to live out the faith in daily life. She received his fatherly advice and instruction, but, even more, she learned by his holy example.

One day, while hearing confessions in the local cathedral, Father Schwind suffered a heart attack. A friend who witnessed the priest in distress summoned Edith. She immediately hurried to be at his side. By the time she reached the cathedral, however, she learned that Father Schwind, the person who had guided her steps as she journeyed into the Catholic Church, had passed away. Edith prayed next to him and accompanied the medical personnel as they carried her dear friend from the cathedral.

Though she found it difficult to put into words the loss she felt, Edith wrote a powerful, heartfelt obituary. She praised Father Schwind's brilliant mind, compassionate heart, and ability to give advice well suited to each person as he bowed in humility before God, respecting God's relationship with the individual soul. Edith explained: "He relied upon his deep knowledge of human beings and his years of apostolic experience, yet his penetration remained gentle through utter reverence before the workings of God's grace in the soul."[66]

Soon after Father Schwind's death, Edith came under the direction of Archabbot Raphael Walzer of the Benedictine Monastery of Beuron, a place Edith had come to love as a silent refuge for her private retreats, particularly during Holy Week. Like Father Schwind, Archabbot Walzer discouraged Edith from entering a cloistered convent.

During the eleven years she waited for her religious vocation to become a reality, Edith followed the advice of her spiritual directors as she also learned to listen quietly to the promptings of the Holy Spirit. She knew that

> the divine light, the Holy Spirit, has never ceased to illumine the darkness of the fallen world.... The silent working of the Holy Spirit in the depths of the soul made the patriarchs into friends of God. However, when they came to the point of allowing themselves to be used as his pliant instruments, he established them in an external visible efficacy....[67]

Edith treasured her friendship with God and was happy to be his "pliant instrument," allowing herself to be led by him into a deeper relationship with the Trinity and into closer relationships with others. It seemed that the more she grew in her love of the Father, Son, and Holy Spirit, the more she grew close to friend and stranger alike.

Gifted with a great capacity for making friends and sustaining relationships through various stages and challenges, Edith showered others with loving concern. In her early twenties, Edith was prompted to consider friendship's role in the battle against evil. Now she would focus on its role in the journey toward intimacy with God. Her circle of friends was like a symphony, each one bringing different gifts and all working together to the glory of God, helping one another along a spiritual journey of joys and sorrows.

Realizing that she could not keep up with all her friends and acquaintances, Edith relied on prayer to keep her connected with them:

> The circle of persons whom I consider as connected with me has increased so much in the course of the years that it is entirely impossible to keep in touch by the usual means. But I have other ways and means of keeping the bonds alive.[68]

Even when she was in the convent, Edith was aware of the troubles and trials facing her friends. She could share her gift of presence with them, though she was not physically present, by pouring out her concern and understanding in letters and praying for their intentions. With characteristic compassion and self-sacrificial love, Edith once explained how badly she felt that she could not spend more time commiserating with a troubled friend:

> ...I could do nothing more than to offer for you all that the rest of the day brought. Only at night did I have

time and quiet to think back upon your affairs; since then they have not let go of me; maybe in that way I am being allowed to share in the weight of your burden.[69]

"Allowed to share" in another's suffering? For Edith, it was a privilege to be able to enter into another's suffering, and she therefore allowed her heart to remain open to another's grief. Continuing on her way in the world, she drew ever closer to God and to so many people she knew God had brought into her life. She was convinced that they were in her life so that she could introduce them to divine life. Her efforts would not succeed without fervent prayer and the grace of the sacraments, particularly the Eucharist. Just as the Eucharistic Lord drew her like a magnet during her days of searching for the truth, so, too, was he drawing her to his Real Presence. As Edith allowed herself to be led to this presence and nourished by God himself, she worked to make his presence known in a world that seemed lost, drifting from his life and love.

CHAPTER 3

Loving with His Love: The Importance of the Eucharist

When Edith was a young child, she would say to her sister as they prepared to go for a walk, "Today, let's go where we have never been before."[1] Years later, Edith demonstrated the same spirit of adventure when it came to her spiritual journey. It was as though she were saying to God, "Today, let's go where we have never been before." She believed God responded to her desire by drawing her closer to his heart, guiding her steps, surprising her with new people, places, events, and situations. God surprised her, too, by introducing her to his hidden life, helping her to discover and to be empowered by his great love. She recognized that the sacraments, particularly the sacrament of love, the Eucharist, had the power to lift her close to his heart, so that she could love with his love. The sacraments allowed her to be carried, not *away*, but toward the places where she could be most effective.

Each new day promised an ever-deepening relationship with God, each morning an opportunity to respond
to his invitation to draw closer. Edith trusted that each
day would bear fruit because God would give her his
grace to start the morning under his guidance and
would empower her to finish the day with the same
focus with which she had begun. Edith never took new
beginnings for granted; and therefore she embraced the
beginning of a new day as a privilege. She said:

> My life begins anew each morning, and ends every
> evening; I have neither plans nor prospects beyond it;
> i.e., to plan ahead could obviously be part of one's daily
> duties—teaching school, for example, could be impossi-
> ble without that—but it must never turn into a "worry"
> about the coming day.[2]

Beginning every day in prayer, Edith calmly surrendered all cares to God. This quiet time with him enabled her, with a sense of passion and authenticity, to
advise others to adopt the same practice. She urged her
audiences to begin their morning attentive to God's
presence and to his call for their lives for that particular day.

Edith cherished the early morning hours, when she
would gaze silently at the tabernacle as she prepared to
participate in the Mass and receive Christ in the
Eucharist. She recognized that "this divine life itself is
the inner driving power from which acts of love come
forth."[3] She encouraged:

> Whoever wants to preserve this life continually within
> herself must nourish it constantly from the source
> whence it flows without end—from the holy sacraments,
> above all from the sacrament of love.... Only in daily,

confidential relationship with the Lord in the tabernacle can one forget self, become free of all one's own wishes and pretentions, and have a heart open to all the needs and wants of others.[4]

Receiving God's life and love in the Eucharist helped Edith to see differently, allowing her to gaze as with God's compassionate eyes upon all those with whom she came into contact. She was able, like Mary at Cana, to see who needed her help—indeed, who needed God's help. She responded with kindness to the student who wanted encouragement, the novice who asked for spiritual counsel, the friend who came to her for marital advice, the stranger who begged for money, and to all who needed a smile or an encouraging word.

Vocation of the Catholic Woman: Fostering a Eucharistic Life

Edith realized that with God's grace she was growing in her spiritual life and she was changing the way she viewed and experienced her Catholic faith. As the years passed, she deepened her understanding of the meaning of living a committed Christian life. With the fervor and excitement of her conversion, Edith wanted—and was ready—"to give up all that was secular and to live totally immersed in thoughts of the Divine."[5] She did not consider this a sacrifice; she yearned for solitary time with God. She did not want to give God only a part of herself or a part of the day; she was prepared to give her entire life.

Slowly she recognized that with this total commitment came a serious responsibility. She explained:

... [G]radually I realized that something else is asked of us in this world...I even believe that the deeper one is drawn into God, the more one must "go out of oneself"; that is, one must go to the world in order to carry the divine life into it.[6]

Edith understood that God invites us to participate in his divine life, and, when we respond in humility and with an open heart to his call, he draws us closer to him. God then calls us out of ourselves to serve him and all those he has entrusted to our care. The more Edith embraced Christ's invitation to intimacy, the more she embraced his call to carry his life to the world.

In September 1930, Edith delivered a talk, "Ethos of Women's Professions" at a convention of Catholic academics in Salzburg, Austria. She stressed the importance of the Eucharist in a woman's life. Underlying the instruction was Edith's own clear love of the Eucharistic Lord:

> Whoever seeks to consult with the Eucharistic God in all her concerns, whoever lets herself be purified by the sanctifying power coming from the sacrifice at the altar, offering herself to the Lord in this sacrifice, whoever receives the Lord in her soul's innermost depth in Holy Communion cannot but be drawn ever more deeply and powerfully into the flow of divine life, incorporated into the Mystical Body of Christ, her heart converted to the likeness of the divine heart.[7]

She continued:

> Something else is closely related to this. When we entrust all the troubles of our earthly existence confidently to the divine heart, we are relieved of them. Then our soul is free to participate in divine life. Then we walk by the side of the Savior on the path that he

traveled on this earth during his earthly existence and still travels in his mystical afterlife. Indeed, with the eyes of faith, we penetrate into the secret depths of his hidden life within the pale of the godhead. On the other hand, this participation in divine life has a liberating power in itself; it lessens the weight of our earthly concerns and grants us a bit of eternity even in this finitude, a reflection of beatitude, a transformation into light. But the invitation to this transformation in God's hand is given to us by God himself in the liturgy of the Church. Therefore, the life of an authentic Catholic woman is also a liturgical life. Whoever prays together with the Church in spirit and in truth knows that her whole life must be formed by this life of prayer.[8]

This life of prayer is a gift from God that helps to build his Mystical Body. The deeper the soul moves into a prayerful relationship with God, the more the soul wishes to express that prayer in the liturgical life of the Church. The soul also is propelled from prayer into service to the members of the Mystical Body. Edith explained this powerfully in her 1930 lecture, "Principles of Women's Education." Here, she described the soul's relationship to the Mystical Body of Christ:

Wherever the soul is enkindled [by God], that soul itself longs for action; and it eagerly grasps the forms of practical life for which God and Holy Church have provided: participation in the Holy Sacrifice of the Mass, a participation which consummates the holy sacrifice *as* an offering in union with the Eucharistic Lord, festive praise of God, and all works of love in which Christ is served in the members of his Mystical Body.[9]

These words reflected a noticeable deepening of Edith's understanding of the power of the Eucharist and of prayer in a busy person's life. It is interesting to recall again how Edith, as a college student, was moved by the sight of the woman with a market basket in the cathedral, as if she were there "for an intimate conversation." Edith was impressed that this woman would come out of the world of daily chores and challenges into the silence of the cathedral, "although no other person was in it...."[10] Edith was struck by the woman walking into the church, but did she see the woman finish praying, stand up, and leave? Did Edith ever imagine the woman resuming her daily activities and encountering the same challenges she had before prayer, but now perhaps faced with renewed energy, having received strength and assistance from God?

Edith had come to appreciate that leading a Eucharistic life means more than removing oneself from the world in order to pray before the tabernacle. This, of course, is crucial, but Edith also understood that the Eucharist helped her to return to the world. Her demanding schedule never kept her away from daily Mass; indeed, it drew her like a magnet toward the Eucharist. She realized that the only way to keep up the hectic pace of her daily life and remain joyful and calm was to begin each day in silent recollection and to receive the power of the Eucharist. From the time of her First Communion, she attended Mass every day, growing in her love of the Eucharist and appreciating the time spent alone with God. She understood that her time in church was not for herself alone, but for her neighbor as well. She therefore urged a friend: "Go right ahead and allow yourself as much time in church as you need in order to find rest and peace. That will not only benefit you, but also your work and all the people with whom you deal."[11]

With confidence in the fruits of the daily reception of the Eucharist, Edith explained the importance of surrendering to God daily: "I will tackle the day's work which he charges me with, and he will give me the power to accomplish it."

> So I will go to the altar of God. Here it is not a question of my minute, petty affairs, but of the great offering of my reconciliation. I may participate in that, purify myself and be made happy, and lay myself with all my doings and troubles along with the sacrifice on the altar. And when the Lord comes to me then in Holy Communion, then I may ask him, "Lord, what do you want of me?" (St. Teresa).[12]

Edith listened astutely and carefully, and she was convinced of God's answer: Before all else, he wanted her heart. He would nourish her heart with his love and empower her to work to build his kingdom on earth.

Having received God in the Eucharist, Edith would spend time in "quiet dialogue" with him and listen more intently to his word within her. Her daily work beckoned, but now it could begin with a renewed sense of joy and commitment. She explained:

> I will still be joyful when I enter into my day's work after this morning's celebration: my soul will be empty of that which could assail and burden it, but it will be filled with holy joy, courage, and energy. Because my soul has left itself and entered into the divine life, it has become great and expansive. Love burns in it like a composed flame which the Lord has enkindled, and which urges my soul to render love and to inflame love in others....[13]

Leading a Eucharistic life, then, points to the unfolding of the divine love story. Edith knew it was a story to be shared with others. Indeed it was a love to be shared, for the closer one is to God, "the more one has to go out of oneself to bring divine life into the world." For Edith, the Eucharistic Lord, Love himself, gives the soul divine love, and this love cannot, by its very nature, be contained. It is like a flame that naturally spreads. The soul therefore needs to come out of itself, fanning the flames of love. Edith realized that the intense flames of divine love not only urge the soul to be loving, that is, to extend love to others, but they also have power to "inflame love in others." Human love becomes fruitful when it collaborates with God's love, when it allows itself to be touched and transformed by God's heart. The soul then is "lifted out of the narrowness of its individual, personal orbit. The concerns of the Lord and his kingdom become the soul's concerns...."[14]

With loving concern, Edith could see the plight of the individual as well as the chaos of the world at large. What she saw, she took to her heart, trying to discern how she could best help. She would rely all the more on her conversations with Jesus in the Eucharist, consulting with his heart beating in the tabernacle.

Her great love of the Eucharist presented a challenge during vacations to her mother's home. She knew that she would long for daily Mass and would miss time spent close to the Eucharistic Lord. Not wanting to hurt her mother by practicing her Catholic faith so openly, Edith developed a plan to go secretly to a nearby church in the early morning hours, before Frau Stein usually would awake. Every morning, Edith quietly left the house to attend Mass at St. Michael the Archangel Church, and then she quietly returned to the house and slipped into her room. When her mother arose, Edith pretended to do the same. It seemed like a fool-proof plan, and its apparent success pleased Edith. However, her mother was more savvy than Edith surmised, for Frau Stein later confided to a friend that she knew full well what was happening but let Edith have her secret.

Transitions: Drawing on the Power of the Eucharist

By the spring of 1931, Edith's work schedule had become unrelenting as she continued to accept invitations to lecture. She also was busy researching a major philosophical project, titled "Potency and Act." Immersing herself in the study of Thomas Aquinas, she realized her teaching was interfering with this important undertaking. There simply was not enough time in the day. Edith brought her problem to the superior of St. Magdalena's, and she received sympathetic support. She was immediately released from her teaching responsibilities.[15] Edith completed the school year and, on the final day of classes, packed and returned to her mother's home. This was not an easy transition. As much as she enjoyed being with her family, she missed convent life. She longed all the more to join the cloistered Carmelites. Early the following year, Edith accepted a teaching position at the German Institute for Scientific Pedagogy in Münster. She made plans to live at the Collegium Marianum with the Sisters of Notre Dame.

Before doing so, Edith renewed her pleas to her spiritual director to allow her to apply to the Carmelites. She explained:

> I had urgently pleaded for permission to enter the order. It was denied me with reference to my mother and because of the effectiveness which my work had had in Catholic circles in recent years. I had yielded.[16]

The answer was still the same: Edith should stay in the secular world.

As with her time at St. Magdalena's, Edith immersed herself in prayer. One young woman recalled, "Frequently I came across her in the chapel...sunk deep in prayer. It was a moving experience to see her there, so completely absorbed in God that nothing could disturb or distract her."[17]

Sometimes, she participated at Mass more than once a day, "kneeling reverently upright, never leaning, never sitting. And at every Mass she followed every prayer of the priest with the greatest devotion. During the day, too, she would visit the Savior in the Eucharist."[18]

For the time being, Edith embraced the role of apprentice, clearly appreciative of the reality of "living under the same roof" as the Eucharistic Lord.[19] Trained as a philosopher to concentrate, ponder, and delve deeply, Edith now was able to lose herself in contemplation, completely focused on the presence of Christ in the Eucharist. She finally had found a definitive answer to her question as a college student, "Is there a personal God?" Not only could she give a heartfelt "yes," but she could also add that this personal God desired her friendship.

She responded to God's invitation with a loving commitment to draw closer to him, a commitment that required disciplined prayer, uninterrupted silence, and time before the tabernacle. It also required utter humility and self-surrender, two traits that seemed to epitomize Edith's deepening spiritual life.

Edith kept her goal of joining the Carmelites close to her heart as she diligently pursued academic work. Her teaching career flourished. She spent time with her students not only in the classroom, but also during their recreation, often joining their games and their casual conversation. With her usual sense of adventure, she arranged class trips, accompanying the young women to museums and the theater. One student vividly remembered Edith bringing them to see a play: "It was Shakespeare's *Hamlet.* We saw the play through her eyes, for she had thrown open the great English dramatist's world to us."[20]

Edith did more than open the world of English literature to her students; she opened to them the world of faith by her words, actions, and, most particularly, her silent prayer. Just as Edith was once inspired by the woman with a market basket praying before the Blessed Sacrament, so, too, were these young women inspired as they watched Edith take time from her daily responsibilities to speak with God. One student attested:

> We saw her every day at Mass up front in the chapel on her kneeler, and we began to get an inkling of what it means to bring faith and conduct into perfect harmony. To us at that critical age she provided an example simply by her bearing. I would not be able to repeat a single thing she said, not so much because it has not stayed

in my memory as because she was a still and silent person who led us only by what she *was*.[21]

Edith seemed to be living out her own words of advice to a fellow teacher:

> Surely the children who attend convent schools should gain there the strength to form their lives in the spirit of Christ. Surely it is most important that the teachers truly have this spirit themselves and vividly exemplify it.[22]

Edith's silence and stillness before the Eucharist spoke volumes about her inner life. It awed those who observed her. Perhaps they felt as though they were daring to approach the threshold of a mystery unfolding before their eyes. Certainly, they considered the inner life of this brilliant philosopher, but also the reality of a living God. One woman remembered, "To see her praying in church, where she often knelt motionless for hours at a time, besides the times of the services, was an impressive sermon."[23]

When Edith stepped away from academia for vacations and retreats, particularly during Advent and Lent, she often visited the Beuron Monastery, a place she found conducive to silent prayer. During Holy Week of 1928, another person observed Edith as "the first to appear in choir, usually before four in the morning... radiant and full of warmth."[24] Her joy on Easter Sunday prompted the witness to wonder "how deeply she must have descended into the godforsakenness and sufferings of the God-man, so as to shine with such Easter brightness."[25]

Edith continued to travel, giving and attending lectures, always managing to find time to enter a church to pray. While in Paris at a philosophical congress on

Phenomenology and Thomism, she took a break to pray with colleagues at the Sacré-Coeur Basilica. A few months later, in December 1932, Edith visited the Ursuline convent in Dorsten, Germany, to celebrate Christmas with the Sisters there. Mother Petra Brüning remembered Edith's long vigil in the chapel:

> On Christmas Eve she joined us in singing matins; then we went to rest for a few hours until midnight. When I returned to the church I found her kneeling motionless in the same position as we had left her; she then attended Mass and sang the office of lauds with us. When I asked her later whether she had not been weary, her eyes lit up and she replied: *"How could this night make one weary?"*[26]

More than fifteen years had elapsed since Edith and her friend had tried to attend Midnight Mass only to find the doors locked. She had left the church disappointed, still searching for the truth, searching for a "personal God." Now it was as if she were voluntarily and happily locked in the church. She would not budge from prayer, never growing tired even after kneeling in the same place for hours.

Her prayers of petition would multiply in the new year as Germany came under the control of the National Socialists. Anti-Semitic measures threatened many of Edith's loved ones. Edith, too, would not escape Nazi persecution. Her lecturing and teaching career in Germany ended abruptly. Could she now finally embrace her calling to Carmel? She would not take any steps before she turned to prayer.

Edith would not simply cry out to God for help; she would have a lengthy conversation with him. On the

Feast of the Good Shepherd, April 30, 1933, Edith entered St. Ludger's Church for this dialogue with God. Here, the parish was observing thirteen hours of prayer for the intercession of St. Ludger. Upon entering the church, Edith promised herself: "I'm not leaving here until I have a clear-cut assurance whether I may now enter Carmel."[27] When the prayer service concluded, Edith was certain she had "the assurance of the Good Shepherd."[28]

With renewed confidence, Edith returned home and immediately wrote a letter of request to her spiritual director, Archabbot Raphael Walzer. By mid-May, she received his permission to apply to enter Carmel. Finally, her years of waiting seemed to be coming to an end. Archabbot Walzer later noted Edith's joy as she

> simply ran to Carmel like a child into its mother's arms.... Carmel had for long been her love and her dream. Once the situation in the Third Reich made it impossible for me to deter her any longer from entering, she simply wished to realize this dream. She heard the voice of the All High, followed it, and did not ask for long where the road led.[29]

Steps Toward Carmel: Relying on the Eucharist

After receiving Archabbot Walzer's permission, Edith took preliminary steps to apply, each step deeply rooted in prayer. She immediately arranged to meet with Dr. Elisabeth Cosack, an acquaintance in Cologne who had close ties to the Carmel there. Arriving in Cologne, Edith participated in Mass at the chapel of the Carmelite convent with her friend Hedwig Spiegel, a recent convert preparing for her Baptism with Edith's guidance. After Mass, Edith met with Dr. Cosack and, during a long walk, explained her desire to become a Carmelite Sister. Dr. Cosack supported her decision and offered to help. She advised Edith that the Carmelites were planning to build a new Carmel in Breslau, close to her mother's home. For Edith this news came as more than a nice surprise; could it be "a sign from heaven"?[30]

Then Dr. Cosack accompanied Edith back to the Carmelite convent, where Edith knelt down at an altar of St. Thérèse of Lisieux. Here, she "experienced the serenity of someone who has reached her goal."[31]While Edith prayed, Dr. Cosack discussed Edith's possible religious vocation with one of the Carmelite Sisters and then with the Mother Prioress, Sister Mary Josepha of the Blessed Sacrament. After their conversation, Dr. Cosack confided to Edith that her dream would likely become a reality. She instructed Edith to return after vespers to speak with the prioress.

Eagerly awaiting the meeting, Edith returned to the chapel much earlier and prayed fervently. After participating in vespers and May devotions, she met with the prioress and the mistress of novices, Sister Teresia Renata de Spiritu Sanctu. When Edith described her spiritual journey and her long desire for Carmel, Sister Teresia echoed the concern Edith often had heard from her spiritual directors: "Could she take responsibility for removing someone from the outside world who could yet accomplish much there?"[32]

The Carmelite provincial would make the decision. Edith would have to meet with him another day.

Edith found it difficult to wait for the provincial's invitation, all the more so because of her concerns for her family, her livelihood, and the political situation. She again entered a church to pray—this time in the cathedral in Münster where she had become a familiar sight. On the Feast of Pentecost, Edith prayed for an answer to her petition to enter Carmel. Feeling prompted by the Holy Spirit, she later wrote to Sister Mary Josepha and soon received an invitation to meet with the vicar for religious. During this interview, the vicar expressed reservations, but still gave Edith the impression she would be accepted. Soon after the meeting, she received a telegram containing four words that would signify a new beginning: "Joyful assent. Regards, Carmel."[33]

Edith immediately went to church to thank God that her years of waiting were over. She would not take her religious vocation for granted, however, and asked friends for their prayers. To one friend she wrote, "Please help me that I may become worthy to live in the inner sanctum of the Church and to represent those who must labor outside."[34]

Before joining Carmel, she would live for a time as a visitor at the convent, followed by two months at her mother's home. During her stay at the convent, she visited often with Hedwig Spiegel, accepting her invitation to be her godmother. Edith attended her friend's Baptism on August 1, and the following day Edith watched her friend receive First Holy Communion in the Carmelites' convent chapel.

As the move to her mother's home drew closer, Edith prayed for strength. Other than her sister Rosa, none of

her family, including her mother, knew of Edith's intention to enter the Carmelites. She met with her spiritual
director on August 10 in Trier and received his blessing
for what would be a difficult time at home. At the cathedral of Trier, Edith prayed before the Holy Robe, vener-
ated as the garment Jesus wore before his crucifixion.
She also prayed at St. Matthew's Church before heading
home. Relying on the Eucharistic Lord would be all the
more imperative in the difficult weeks ahead in Breslau.

At home, Edith confided in her sister Rosa, who lent
a sympathetic ear. For many years Rosa had wanted to be
baptized a Catholic, but did not do so in deference to
her mother. Still no one suspected that Edith would be
joining the Carmelites. Frau Stein was heartened that
Edith had returned to Breslau and confided in her
daughter all her worries about the political situation,
lamenting bitterly that "there are such wicked people in
the world."[35]

Frau Stein was upset because her daughter Erna and
her family were preparing to move to another part of
the city. The move came at a very difficult time. As the
political climate worsened, Frau Stein's business failed
and her home, once full of children and grandchildren,
grew more empty and lonely. Edith knew that she could
not add to her mother's worries. She would wait to
reveal her news and so allow her mother to enjoy their
"cozy togetherness."[36]

At the urging of a priest friend, Edith began to work
on a book to combat caricatures of Judaism. This book
would portray life in a Jewish family, and Edith planned
to tell the story from the perspective of her mother's
life. To do this, Edith sat with her mother as Frau Stein

knitted, and gently prodded her mother for memories of her youth.

The two women bonded all the more as they worked on the book. Though it appeared a scene of contentment, Edith would look at her mother and think, "...if only you knew!"[37] Edith guarded her secret for weeks until her mother unexpectedly and directly asked: "What will you do with the Sisters in Cologne?" Edith answered her mother with equal directness: "Live with them." Edith captured the poignant scene that followed the revelation:

> Now there followed desperate denial. My mother never stopped knitting. Her yarn became tangled: with trembling hands she sought to unravel it, and I helped her as our discussion continued.[38]

The news devastated Frau Stein, who knew she probably would never see her daughter again.

To a friend, Edith referred to

> the great pain that I must be causing her and have before my eyes daily. You will help me, won't you, to beg that my mother will be given the strength to bear the leave-taking, and the light to understand it?[39]

Edith realized that she could not alleviate her mother's burden by human means, but had "firm confidence in God's grace and...the strength of our prayer."[40]

Other family members also found Edith's decision unfathomable. They felt she was abandoning them at a time of great persecution just when they most needed family stability and security. Confronted by her twelve-year-old niece, Susel, who expressed such hurt, Edith held her hand as she calmly clarified the spiritual reasons for her decision. She thought that Susel understood, but Susel later confessed that she and her family still found Edith's move incomprehensible.[41]

In the weeks that followed, Frau Stein, in particular, remained visibly upset, alternating between crying and protesting. When Sister Marianne, one of the Carmelites, came from Cologne to oversee the founding of the new Carmel in Breslau, Frau Stein met with her, hoping she would dissuade Edith from leaving her family. Sister Marianne did not discourage Edith, but neither did she encourage her. Edith understood the challenge of taking sides:

> The decision was so difficult that no one could tell me with certainty which was the right path. Good reasons could be cited for both alternatives. I had to take that step in the complete darkness of faith.[42]

And she had to make the decision alone. She pondered, "Which of us two will break down, my mother or I? But both of us managed to persevere to the last day."[43]

Every morning Edith would leave the house at 5:30 A.M. to attend Mass at the nearby church of St. Michael the Archangel. She lived the words of her lectures of many years before in which she urged people to consult with the Eucharistic Lord daily. She understood the importance of surrendering all her "doings and troubles along with the sacrifice on the altar. And then, when the Lord comes to me in Holy Communion, I may ask him, 'Lord, what do you want of me?'"

Though she had a heavy heart, she remained convinced that God wanted her to join Carmel. The day before she left home, she arose and went to Mass. She then accompanied her mother to synagogue for the Jewish Feast of Tabernacles. Edith enjoyed the sermon and told her mother so as they walked the forty-five minutes home. The conversation that ensued reinforced the religious differences between mother and daughter. Frau Stein asked, "It's possible...to be devout as a Jew also?" Edith replied, "Certainly, if one has not come to know anything else." This would be their last long private conversation, and it culminated in Frau Stein desperately asking: "Why did you have to come to know it? I don't want to say anything against *him*. He may have been a very good man. But why did he make himself into God?"[44]

The conversation affirmed what Edith had come to accept: the Catholic faith was, and would remain, a foreign world to her mother.

> It was totally impossible to make my mother understand anything. Everything remained in all its starkness and incomprehensibility, and I was able to leave only by placing a firm confidence in God's grace and by the strength of our prayer. That my mother, too, has faith, and, finally, that she still has great inner strength made it a little bit easier.[45]

The two women returned home to welcome the visitors who came and went all afternoon and evening to bid farewell. When the last visitor left, Frau Stein sat down and began to weep. Edith held her mother's head close to her heart. After a long period, mother and daughter walked upstairs, and Edith, for the first and last time, helped her mother undress. Then she sat on her mother's bed until Frau Stein encouraged Edith to get some sleep.[46]

After a restless night, Edith went to early morning Mass. The day of great new beginnings would start with the Eucharist. Following Mass, Edith joined her family for breakfast. Her mother grieved inconsolably and could not eat. The scene from the previous night was replayed as Frau Stein sobbed and Edith held her close until it was time to leave. Then Erna held her mother as Edith put on her hat and coat. Frau Stein said her final good-bye with a warm hug, but then cried again as Edith embraced Erna one last time.

Edith's final image of her mother affected her deeply: the heart-wrenching sight of Frau Stein in tears, sobbing uncontrollably. Sorrow had pierced her mother's heart, and Edith knew she had caused it. The burden of separation weighed heavily on both women, a weight almost too difficult to bear.

Edith's sisters Else and Rosa accompanied Edith on the trolley to the train station. The trolley passed Frau Stein's parlor windows—the same parlor where Edith had worked as a young philosopher before her conversion, and where she had hung a picture of St. Francis of Assisi. There Erna had been married twelve years before, and in that room Edith had resolved to take care of her spiritual life. That decision had taken her on a long spiritual journey from agnostic philosopher to Catholic teacher, and it now was leading her to become a cloistered nun.

Usually when the Steins traveled on the trolley, they would gaze in the direction of the family home and see a family member waving from the parlor window. Looking up for that final farewell, Edith was disheartened to see that no one was waving. Frau Stein likely was still crying on Erna's shoulders. Edith arrived at the train station with her sisters, and Else hugged Edith closely as the train arrived. Edith would never again see Else or any other family member except Rosa, who understood Edith's journey and calmly bid her sister farewell. Edith boarded the train, found a seat, and, as the train left the station, waved good-bye until she no longer saw her sisters.

A new life was beginning, but Edith could not feel any "wild joy." She later wrote how "the scene I had just left behind was too terrible for that." She knew the pain she had caused her family and that they were still suffering, yet she still experienced "a deep peace, in the harbor of the divine will."[47] On the journey to Cologne, Edith wrote letters to friends, asking them to pray for and to visit her mother.

Arriving in Cologne, Edith spent the night at the home of her friend Hedwig Spiegel. On the following day, the two women joined the nuns for vespers and then met with the Mistress of Novices, Sister Teresa Renata. Hedwig Spiegel and Sister Teresa accompanied Edith to the door of the cloister. With great anticipation, Edith looked at the door: "At last it opened, and in deep peace I crossed the threshold into the House of the Lord."[48] The darkness of the preceding weeks disappeared, and God's light seemed now to stream forth, directing Edith Stein's new beginning.

Beginnings of Religious Life: Nurturing a Eucharistic Spirituality

When Edith walked through the door of the cloistered convent, she remained committed to the world she seemed to have left behind. She knew that world well and wanted to carry its concerns into the convent. She understood her vocation was "to stand before God for all."[49] Inviting friends to visit her, she hoped she could share the peace she was experiencing. To a college friend Edith offered: "If you are not too far away, you will perhaps visit me sometime, either here or there. I would very much like to share some of the peace that is granted to us with all those I know outside."[50]

As a Carmelite, Edith would be known as Teresa Benedicta of the Cross. Similar to her namesake, Teresa of Avila, Edith continued to find peace particularly in Eucharistic adoration. Soon after she entered Carmel, Edith wrote an essay about St. Teresa that captured the mystic's joy...but it also may point to Edith's own experience of the Eucharist. She wrote:

> With holy joy the young novice participated in choral prayer. But the prescribed prayer times were not sufficient for her zeal. She also was happiest spending her free hours in silent contemplation before the tabernacle.[51]

Edith, too, continued to be drawn to such contemplation, and she encouraged her Carmelite Sisters to find their joy in it as well. She urged that those

> who enter Carmel must give themselves wholly to the Lord. Only one who values her little place in the choir before the tabernacle more highly than all the splendor of the world can live here, can then truly find a joy that no worldly splendor has to offer.[52]

Edith seemed to personify such joy when she wrote to a friend about "a wonderful gift"—that of a tabernacle being built into the choir grate where Edith could see it perfectly as she knelt in the chapel.[53]

In quiet adoration, Edith remembered in prayer the needs of those outside Carmel, and all the troubles that people brought to her attention in letters and in personal visits. She explained to one person who brought prayer requests:

> Intentions such as yours are not out of the ordinary for us. Similar ones are brought daily to our door or come in the mail. After all, it is our profession to pray, and many people rely on that. We all pray in common, daily, for the intentions commended to us, and each one adds to that her own contribution for those who are especially under her care.[54]

When people brought their cares and concerns directly to the convent, they would be directed to the cloister's grilled window, where they could converse with a particular Sister. Edith confessed that she felt awkward during these meetings; they were

> like a transition into a strange world, and we are happy to flee once more into the silence of the choir and, before the tabernacle, to ponder over those matters that have been entrusted to us.[55]

Retreating to the peace behind the cloistered gate was not an escape route to self-centered concerns. Edith noted:

> ...I still regard this peace, daily, as an immense gift of grace that has not been given for one's own exclusive benefit. And when someone comes to us worn out and crushed and then takes away a bit of rest and comfort, that makes me very happy.[56]

She gave visitors something of the divine peace she was experiencing, and they, in turn, carried this into the world.

She was happy to know of this type of supernatural effect, explaining, "The confidence that something of our peace and our silence flows out into the world, and supports those who are still on pilgrimage, is the only thing that can reassure me when I consider that I, rather than so many more worthy ones, have been called into this wonderful security."[57]

Visitors also came to pray with the Sisters, as Edith described in an essay on St. Teresa of Avila. She wrote:

Yesterday in our monastery church we had perpetual adoration [forty-hours devotion]. On such days, the faithful who are associated with our Carmel gather around the altar singing and praying from about six o'clock in the morning until ten o'clock at night. Then the church is closed and during the night the sisters take turns keeping watch in the choir before the Blessed Sacrament.... By their steadfast supplications, they draw God's grace and mercy on a humanity submerged in sin and need. In our time, when the powerlessness of all natural means for battling the overwhelming misery everywhere has been demonstrated so obviously, an entirely new understanding of the power of prayer, of expiation, and of vicarious atonement has again awakened.[58]

Edith's prayer life seemed to have the effect of deepening her humility all the more. When she received thanks for her prayers, she responded:

It is often a real source of embarrassment for us when people credit us with special effectiveness in prayer, or with holiness. We can detect nothing extraordinary about ourselves. Despite that it does seem that the Lord gladly helps those who turn to us. It is probably the reward of their confidence, perhaps also the return for our having given ourselves to him. But if the prayer is to

be effective for you, then you have to do your part
also....[59]

Just as Edith was ill at ease with all the accolades she
received on the lecture circuit, she was even more
uncomfortable with the praise she received in the convent. She protested vigorously any suggestion that she
and the Sisters were somehow better than those outside
the cloistered walls. To a woman who lavished compliments on Edith and the Sisters, Edith responded kindly
but firmly:

> I do not want to sadden you at all, but I think I must
> mention something about your last letter, as about many
> previous ones, that caused me some distress. This is your
> inference that there is an apparently tremendous differ-
> ence between you and me.... I should consider myself a
> Pharisee if I were to accept such assurances in silence,
> because they have no objective foundation. You are by
> no means the only person in whom our grille instills a
> pious awe. But this grille does not mean that on that
> side—"in the world"—everything is wicked, whereas on
> this side everything is perfect. We know how much
> human poverty still lies concealed below the habit, and
> therefore it is very embarrassing for us whenever we
> find someone strewing incense. God is merciful and
> kindhearted beyond all conception and already rewards
> in incomparable measure the mere intention of conse-
> crating oneself entirely to him. When you are here you
> experience in some way the peace of his house, and this
> we are happy to share with you wholeheartedly. But you
> must not attribute to a poor human being what is, in
> fact, God's gift.[60]

Edith was grateful to God for many gifts, including
the grace of her vocation and her many friendships, but
most particularly for the gift of his divine life. On the

Feast of Corpus Christi, 1935, Edith wrote a poem for
Sister Maria on the day she took her vows as a Carmelite.
In this gift to her friend, she pondered the gift of God's
friendship in the Eucharist:

> This Heart, it beats for us in a small tabernacle
> Where it remains mysteriously hidden
> In that still, white host.
> That is your royal throne on earth, O Lord....
> Full of love, you sink your gaze into mine.[61]

Edith had grown tremendously in her understanding
of the Eucharist since the time she had observed the
woman stopping into church as if to speak with a friend.
Edith now knew that Jesus was truly present, and she was
convinced that as she gazed upon him, he was returning
the gaze with love.

While time spent in such intimate Eucharistic prayer
allowed Edith's relationship with Jesus to blossom, Edith
knew that he still wanted to draw even closer to her. She
had said so beautifully many years earlier that: "...who-
ever receives the Lord in her soul's innermost depth in
Holy Communion cannot but be drawn ever more
deeply and powerfully into the flow of divine life, incor-
porated into the Mystical Body of Christ, her heart converted to the likeness of the divine heart."[62] Now in the
convent, she addressed Jesus in poetic form using the
first person:

> You come to me as early morning's meal each
>   daybreak...
> Your body mysteriously permeates mine
> And your soul unites with mine:
> I am no longer what once I was....
> There remains the bond that binds heart to heart,

> The stream of life that springs from yours
> And animates each limb.[63]

Christ's heart that "beats for us in a small tabernacle" now comes into the soul where it animates the soul to love. Edith knew that God was not only guiding her steps, taking her to places she had never been before, but he was also transforming her life, enabling her to "become someone," that is, the person he intended her to be: his beloved child, and his trusted collaborator in building his kingdom.

It is interesting to recall how, many years before, Edith took exception to a friend's comment that she had "become someone" because of all her lectures. Edith would not hear of it. Countless compliments on her lectures did not make her "someone." She would be open to transformation, but only by her Creator!

In her 1936 essay, "The Prayer of the Church," Edith also emphasized the transforming power of the Mass, explaining:

> The sacrifice itself is a sacrifice of expiation that transforms the faithful as it transforms the gifts, unlocks heaven for them, and enables them to sing a hymn of praise pleasing to God.[64]

With a profound sense of awe, Edith elaborated that the Eucharist

> is itself the bread of life that we need daily to grow into eternal life. It makes our will into an instrument at God's disposal. Thereby it lays the foundation for the kingdom of God in us.... Participation in the sacrifice and in the sacrificial meal actually transforms the soul into a living stone in the city of God—in fact, each individual soul into a temple of God.[65]

Edith clearly appreciated the ineffable nature of the Eucharist. Indeed, in concluding her poem on the Eucharist, the woman of great intellect, of lofty and profound sentiments, seemed at a loss for words before the mystery of the Blessed Sacrament:

> How wonderful are your gracious wonders!
> All we can do is be amazed and stammer and fall silent
> Because intellect and words fail.[66]

Terror-Filled Times: Clinging to the Eucharist

Edith's love of the Eucharistic God became all the more obvious as Germany bowed under the control of the National Socialists. Concerned about her loved ones, she intensified her prayers. She also began to consider the real possibility that she might be taken from the convent because of her Jewish heritage. In her work on John of the Cross, she alluded to the pain of being deprived of the Eucharist, emphasizing how the saint could not celebrate Mass or receive Communion during his imprisonment. It was as though Edith were bracing herself for her own imprisonment. She encouraged the Sisters to develop their Eucharistic lives, explaining:

> For us [the sacraments] are the prescribed means to grace, and we cannot receive them eagerly enough. But God is not bound to them. At the moment when some external force were to cut us off from receiving the sacraments, he could compensate us, superabundantly, in some other way; and he will do so all the more certainly and generously the more faithfully we have adhered to the sacraments previously.[67]

This "external force" was becoming all the more real and sinister with each passing year. In November 1938, the Nazis terrorized and assaulted Jewish people in Germany on Kristallnacht. This threatened Edith's own safety, and her superiors quickly made plans for her move to a Carmel in Echt, Holland. As she prepared to leave the convent, an elderly Sister tearfully thanked Edith for the model she had been to the Sisters. Edith responded with humility and gratitude: "It is I who must thank God for having allowed me to live with you."[68]

Edith brought the same grateful spirit to her new home in Echt, where she moved on New Year's Day 1939. She also brought her courage, for she sensed that she would not remain safe for long. She said:

> My basic attitude is one of gratitude—grateful that I may be here and that the house is as it is. At the same time I always have a lively awareness that we do not have a lasting city here. I have no other desire than that God's will be done in me and through me.... But much prayer is necessary in order to remain faithful in all situations. Especially [must we pray] for those who have heavier burdens to carry than I have, and who are not so rooted in the Eternal. Therefore I am sincerely grateful to all who help.[69]

She surrendered to God's plan and trusted that he would always carry her.

As Edith's prayer life intensified, she continued to receive the nourishment of God's word. She grew to appreciate the relationship of the Eucharist to Scripture, emphasizing that

> the same Savior, whom the written word presents to our eyes on all the paths he trod on earth in human form,

lives among us disguised in the form of the eucharistic bread. He comes to us every day as the bread of life. In either of these forms, he is near to us; in either of these forms he wants to be sought and found by us.[70]

She, who once considered Bach her "daily bread," now was nourished by God's word in Scripture and his life in the Eucharist.

Edith understood that the more we read Scripture, the more we long for his life in the Eucharist, and the more we receive the sacrament of love, the more we wish to know the word of God. "The one supports the other," she wrote.

> When we see that Savior before us with the eyes of faith as the Scriptures portray him, then our desire to receive him in the bread of life increases. The eucharistic bread, on the other hand, awakens our desire to get to know the Lord in the written word more and more deeply and strengthens our spirit to get a better understanding.[71]

At the beginning of 1941 (the year before she was killed), as the war escalated, Edith again contemplated the role of the Eucharist. On January 6, she wrote:

> A new year at the hand of the Lord—we do not know whether we shall experience the end of this year. But if we drink from the fount of the Savior each day, then each day will lead us deeper into eternal life and prepare us to throw off the burdens of this life easily and cheerfully at some time when the call of the Lord sounds.[72]

Drawing close to the word of God in Scripture and the Eucharist, Edith was ready to follow him as she asked, "Lord, what do you want from me?" She was ready to continue the spiritual adventure of going where she had never been before, and she recognized that God might ask her to go where his presence was hidden. She was prepared to respond as Mary did, with a ready fiat, her "yes" to God's plan, wherever that might lead.

A family portrait of the Steins was taken in 1895. Since Siegfried Stein, Edith's father (third from left, back row), had died suddenly the year before, the family had his passport photo inserted into the picture. Shown are (from left, back row) Arno, Else, Siegfried, Elfriede, Paul; front row: Rosa, Auguste, Edith, and Erna.

The youngest of the family, Edith (right) shared a close friendship with her sister Erna.

The Stein home at Michaelistrasse 38 in Breslau, acquired by Frau Stein in 1910. Family members can be seen at the windows of the second floor.

Yearning for greater independence, in May of 1906 Edith Stein left for Hamburg to stay for a time with her sister Else and to help with her two small children. Edith (left) with Else and her second child, Werner.

Shown here with a group of friends and her sister Erna (right), Edith (below) enjoyed nature and hiking. This photo was probably taken during the summer of 1911.

Adolf Reinach and his wife, Anna, became dear friends of Edith Stein, and they played a significant role in her conversion. Anna's strength and Christian courage in the face of her husband's death during World War I inspired Edith immensely.

Edith (foreground) was a Red Cross nurse at a military hospital. There she came face to face with the reality of terrible suffering and death.

In Göttingen, Edith became terribly frustrated and disillusioned while working on her thesis, "On the Problem of Empathy." Edith turned to Adolf Reinach, who proved an invaluable help. She said, "I had been rescued from distress by a good angel."

In 1916, Edith and Pauline Reinach, Adolf Reinach's sister, stepped into the Cathedral at Frankfurt. There Edith witnessed a woman praying as if in intimate conversation. The event remained an indelible memory.

Edith also visited the Liebig Museum in Frankfurt. The faces of the sculpted figures shown above so captivated her, she found it difficult to move on.

*Unable to secure a perma-
nent position at a university, Edith returned to the
family home in Breslau,
where the parlor was con-
verted into her office.*

*In the summer of 1921,
Edith visited Hedwig
Conrad-Martius (shown in
her garden), a fellow
philosopher and a recent
convert to Lutheranism.
In her library, Edith
discovered the autobiography of St. Teresa of Avila,
which she devoured in one
night. The book helped her
to decide to become a
Catholic.*

Frau Stein and her grand-daughter, Susanne, Erna's child. Edith bore the heavy weight of knowing how much pain her conversion would cause her mother.

Though Edith felt a strong desire to enter the cloistered Carmelites, her spiritual director and treasured friend, Father Joseph Schwind, vicar general of the Diocese of Speyer, advised her to continue her work in the world.

While living at home with her mother, Edith arose early each morning to attend Mass at the Church of St. Michael the Archangel in Breslau.

Edith had this photo taken in Breslau during the summer vacation of 1916.

Edith with a group of her students at St. Magdalena's school. While teaching there, Edith lived at the Dominican convent and joined the community for prayer and daily Mass.

A photo of Edith taken while she was living in Speyer.

Edith became a popular lecturer on the topic of Christian spirituality, particularly on the vocation of women.

Edith was highly praised for the substance of her lectures as well as her evident humility and authenticity.

Edith Stein, at age 40 (1931), realized that her responsibilities as a teacher and lecturer left her little time for her philosophical project, "Potency and Act." She asked to be relieved of her duties and returned to Breslau at the end of the school year.

The postulant Edith Stein wore a white wedding dress, according to the custom of the time, for the Mass for her entrance into Carmel.

The newly professed wore a crown of white roses. This photo was taken in the garden of the Carmel in Cologne.

This photo shows the enclosed choir where the Carmelite nuns daily prayed their Office and spent hours in contemplation. Here Edith remembered in prayer the needs brought to her attention, and her family and friends.

This photo of Sister Teresa Benedicta of the Cross was taken for her passport, which she needed to leave Germany for the Carmel in Echt, Holland, following the violence of Kristallnacht.

Rosa Stein also converted to Catholicism and moved to the Carmel in Echt. She served the community in many ways, including working in the garden where this photo of the two sisters was taken.

The final photo taken of Edith Stein, probably during the summer of 1942, before her arrest in August.

CHAPTER 4

Carrying Divine Life: The Example of Mary

As Edith continued her Christian journey, she real-ized she had become a stranger to the world, a world that had plummeted into the depths of darkness and sin, far removed from the will of God. She felt apart, but not aloof. With a heightened sense of responsibility, she sought to bring the perfect love and life of Jesus Christ to an imperfect world. Who better to teach her how to carry divine life into that world than the maiden who was the *"gateway through which God found entrance to humankind"*? [1] Who better to guide her steps than "the first Christian to follow Christ, and...the first and most perfect model of Christ"? [2]

Edith relied on Mary's intercession, learned from her example, and strove to imitate her virtues. Like St. Thérèse of Lisieux, Edith loved Mary particularly as Mother.

She believed Mary's maternal intercession helped her to listen to the voice of Christ and to respond to his invitation to intimacy. From Mary, Edith learned the great power of spiritual seeds buried in the depths of a soul's hidden life: seeds of silence, solitude, and prayer. These invisible forces helped Mary to fulfill her mission to be the Mother of the Son of God; these same forces can transform a decaying society into the flourishing kingdom of God. Edith elaborated:

> The work of salvation takes place in obscurity and still-ness. In the heart's quiet dialogue with God the living building blocks out of which the kingdom of God grows are prepared, the chosen instruments for the construction forged.[3]

Mary's "quiet dialogue with God" prepared her for service; indeed, her interior life propelled her into the world.

Edith practiced what she learned, soon realizing that time spent alone with Christ helped her to journey close to his heart and to the heart of the Church. Inspired by Mary's strength, steadfastness, and love, she understood that she, like Mary, was called to stand courageously, fulfilling her vocation with dignity and faithful persever-ance as she embraced Christ's cross.

Edith's Marian focus shaped the advice she gave her students and audiences in both her lectures and essays, and from it flowed the practical way she put her Marian devotion into daily practice.

Edith's Instruction on Mary

Edith made it clear that a relationship with Mary never diverts our gaze from her Son but points the way to him.[4] Mary "loves us, she knows us, she exerts herself to bring each one of us the closest possible relationship with the Lord...."[5] Therefore, we best reciprocate Mary's love by loving her Son and collaborating with him in his redemptive mission.

As "the perfect image of a mother," Mary gives us her example of heartfelt love in action—the mother who sought to protect her Son in his infancy and childhood, who cared for him throughout his earthly life, and collaborated in his work of love.[6] It is work that continues today. Edith emphasized:

> Her service is rendered directly to him: through the prayer of intercession, she intercedes with him for humankind; she receives from his hands graces to be bestowed and does indeed transmit them.[7]

Edith compared Mary's role beside Christ to Eve's role beside Adam, but noted a major difference: while Eve was beside Adam for *his* sake, "Mary is beside Jesus...for ours...her maternal love embraces the whole Mystical Body with Jesus Christ its head."[8]

Marian spirituality, then, is Christocentric and ecclesial. Fostering both contemplation and action, Marian spirituality helps direct our attention to Christ's work in our souls and Christ's invitation to collaborate with him in caring for other souls. In Edith's lectures and in her daily life, she certainly embodied this practical dimension of Marian spirituality.

Less than eight years after her entry into the Catholic Church, Edith accepted an invitation to speak at a convention of Catholic academics held in Salzburg, Austria. The topic of the 1930 convention was "Christ and the Vocational Life of the Modern Person," and Edith focused on "The Ethos of Women's Professions." Her

outline in preparation for this talk gives a glimpse into
her own spiritual life and foreshadows themes in later
lectures, essays, and classroom instructions. The outline
crystallized her purpose—that of demonstrating the
mission of Mary, "Virgin, Mother, and Queen," as it
relates to contemporary women.[9]

Edith emphasized the spiritual tools needed to help
a "depraved era," recognizing that the prescription to
renew the face of the earth is "the renewal of true interior life."[10] This means constant recourse to prayer, liturgy, self-sacrifice, and silence before God.[11] Edith
reminded her audiences: "The decision for the redemption was conceived in the eternal silence of the inner
divine life. The power of the Holy Spirit came over the
Virgin praying alone in the hidden, silent room in
Nazareth and brought about the Incarnation of the
Savior."[12] Silence is life-giving.

Mary, who "kept every word sent from God in her
heart," is our model of silence and humility, the keys to
living out our Christian life whether "in the world" or in
contemplative religious life.[13] Mary teaches us how to
foster silence in our lives so that we may hear God's
voice, recognize his presence, and accept and follow his
instructions. Mary's self-surrender and obedience echo
to us in the few sentences, the "grains of pure gold," that
she uttered as recorded in the Gospels.[14]

The beginning of Mary's conversation with the angel
conveys a lesson about the purity of her intention to
serve God wholeheartedly. Edith emphasized that
Mary's question, "How shall this happen, since I know
not man?"

...is the simple recognition of her *virginal purity*. She had consecrated her whole heart and all the strength of her body, soul, and spirit to the service of God in undivided surrender. Thereby she pleased the Almighty. He accepted her surrender and blessed her with wonderful fruitfulness by raising her to be the Mother of God.[15]

Mary's purity, then, was the seed of her motherhood.

Mary's second word to the angel also points to her pure heart: "...in the statement 'I am the handmaid of the Lord,' Mary's whole being is articulated. It bespeaks her readiness to serve the Lord and excludes every other relationship."[16] It is, after Christ's example, "the most perfect expression of obedience."[17] Mother and Son, then, demonstrated perfect obedience and perfect conformance to the will of the Father.[18]

Mary and Joseph also shared that commitment to fulfilling the Father's will as they embraced their vocations as spouses and parents. Faithful obedience directed the steps of the pregnant Madonna from the security of her home to the unknown world where she gave birth to the Son of God.[19]

Edith encouraged women to follow Mary's example so that, in trustful obedience, they, too, would allow God to lead them into the unknown. Putting their lives in his hands, they become his "flexible instruments...[and effecting] his work to which he leads us. If we fulfill our mission, we do what is best for ourselves, for our immediate environment, and together with it, what is best for the entire nation."[20]

Edith understood that the nation desperately needed souls immersed in deep relationships with God, focused not on their own will but on his. When souls recognize their dependence on God, they readily empty themselves of their self-will and anything that can distract them from the will of God. Without this self-emptying and self-forgetfulness, the soul has no room to welcome God's life. The soul is not ready for the noble task of carrying divine life.

An interior life cultivated by quiet stillness prepares souls to surrender their lives to God and later to venture into the chaotic noise of society, remaining calm and focused. Then they are ready to see more clearly society as it really is in order to renew and transform it. Certainly, Mary is the model for such souls, but many other women in Church history have followed Mary's lead, becoming "totally self-forgetful because they were steeped in the life and suffering of Christ...."[21] These faith-filled women

> were the Lord's preferred choice as instruments to accomplish great things in the Church: a St. Bridget, a Catherine of Siena. And when St. Teresa, the powerful reformer of her Order at a time of widespread falling away from the faith, wished to come to the rescue of the Church, she saw the renewal of true interior life as the means toward this end.[22]

Edith's words seem almost prophetic in light of the 1999 Apostolic Letter of Pope John Paul II, proclaiming Saints Edith, Bridget, and Catherine co-patronesses of Europe.

This "renewal of true interior life" is the key to fulfilling a vocation of Christian leadership. Mary could lead because she could follow. She could be fruitful because she was always empty of self. She could give her "yes" to motherhood because she first had given her "yes" to childhood, that is, her assent as handmaiden. Her ability to recognize herself as handmaiden indicates her childlike humility and her mature readiness to become a mother. Her spiritual childhood necessarily preceded her motherhood.

Edith explained that "motherhood was transfigured" when "God chose as the instrument for his incarnation a human mother...."[23] In that holy motherhood, Mary

> watches over his childhood; near or far, indeed, wherever he wishes, she follows him on his way; she holds the crucified body in her arms; she carries out the will of the departed. But not as *her* action does she do all this: she is in this the handmaid of the Lord; she fulfills that to which God has called her. And that is why she does not consider the child as her own property: she has welcomed him from God's hands; she lays him back into God's hands by dedicating him in the Temple and by being with him at the crucifixion.[24]

Mary's embrace of her vocation to carry divine life did not begin at the moment of Christ's birth, but at the moment she learned that she was to be his mother, long before she saw Jesus with her own eyes. Hidden in Mary's womb, Jesus was protected and nourished by Mary, who with "composed expectancy" blissfully awaited his birth.[25] Looking forward to his birth, she committed herself to his life and his mission. She would not stand in the way of God's plan but would surrender to his will, and

> in a life fully surrendered to service, she takes careful note of all words and signs which anticipate something of his future course. With all reverence for the divinity hidden in him, she still maintains authority over him

when he is a child; in true perseverance, she partici-
pates in his work until his death and beyond it.[26]

Mary's stewardship of Jesus' life and vocation shows
how she treasured her child as a gift "from God for
God," rather than as "a personal possession."[27] Like
Mary, women are called to see their own children as gifts
from God—indeed, all relationships as gifts. Edith
reminded women of their responsibilities to all those
they meet, particularly those whom God entrusted to
their friendship. In Mary, then, we see the beauty of biological and spiritual motherhood.

In Edith's 1932 article, "Woman as Guide in the
Church," she stressed:

> Filled with the spirit of supernatural maternity, woman
> has the mission to win others over as children of God. In
> a particular way, woman is a symbol of the Church, the
> Bride of Christ. Supernatural maternity impregnates
> only women who live and die with Christ, and who awak-
> en through education the same purpose in those
> entrusted to them.[28]

How do women, then, introduce others to Christ,
"win others over as children of God"? They need to con-
tinually make "room within [themselves] for God's
being and works."[29] Once they do this, they can carry
divine life into the world in various ways. First, having
developed a relationship with God in prayer and in participation in the liturgy and the sacramental life of the
Church, they are able to reflect his presence in all that
they do and wherever they go in the world. Second,
being close to the heart of Christ enables them to better
see the image of God in others and to help them to recognize God within themselves. In that way, they truly are

able to "unveil the image of Christ in another." Third, they carry divine life by their ongoing death to self and their willingness to sacrifice daily to let his life shine through them. In giving of themselves, they foster the work of God in society, planting seeds for his divine life to be carried into an era estranged from him. Fourth, they carry divine life in such a way as to introduce others to God's life, and also to ignite a spark of love for God within them, enflaming that love so that this love flies into action for God and neighbor. Fifth, they carry divine life as they foster, sustain, nourish, and protect the life of grace in others, whether their own children, their students, or other adults.

In imitating Mary, women are to watch carefully the conditions in which they find themselves, whether it be in the home, the office, the parish, through public service or indeed wherever they may be serving. They are "to carry the spirit of Christ everywhere."[30] Mary will help them to carry her Son into the world and "to unveil Christ in the heart of another."[31]

To appreciate Mary's "maternal attitude in every situation," Edith encouraged women to consider the images of Mary as the heart of the first Christian community and in her maternal role at Cana.[32] Edith explained that, "motherliness must be that which does not remain within the narrow circle of blood relations or of personal friends; but in accordance with the model of the Mother of Mercy, it must have its root in universal divine love for all who are there, belabored and burdened."[33] Mary's vigilance at Cana points to this type of motherliness. Silently and perceptively, she observes "what is lacking. Before anything is noticed, even before embarrassment sets in, she has procured already the remedy."[34]

Edith, once the young crusader for a woman's right to vote, encouraged, even pleaded with women to become actively involved in confronting the pressing issues of the day.[35]

In her 1928 lecture "The Significance of Women's Intrinsic Value in National Life," Edith urged: "The nation needs [a woman's] services sorely as a *mother* and as a *professional educator* in helping others to attain to total humanity. Such a woman is like a seminal spore bringing new life to the national body."[36] Edith believed women's vocation was not only to be "new life" to the nation, but also to help "unveil" God's life and bring his Holy Spirit into a "depraved era."[37]

The home, the office, the public arena—all these settings may become holy ground, as workers strive to do God's will, to accomplish his work, and to "unveil" his presence. Edith particularly looked to the teaching profession as an opportunity to demonstrate God's love. She understood the power of the teacher who cares for her students as if they were her own children. A teacher

> must further the life of faith by providing a secure and enduring foundation…she must be the maternal, loving educator for Christ. She must nourish a rich life of faith in young persons…. By so consecrating herself to supernatural maternity, the Catholic woman becomes an organ of the Church. And, in this way, she will fulfill this function in the religious life as in a life united to God in the world.[38]

It is not just the teacher in the classroom who exemplifies the "maternal, loving educator for Christ," but all those who strive to help others draw close to God as his children.

With the help of Mary, they may see opportunities to help others and to hear cries of distress and the sometimes muffled sobs.

This work of carrying divine life involves suffering, as Mary's vocation teaches us. Her maternal vocation was lived out in all its eloquence on Golgotha, where, with a broken and pierced heart, she stood in love for her Son and for each one of us. With the "lifeblood of her bitter pains," she collaborated in Christ's redemptive mission. For Edith, Mary's example of such suffering is a role model for all women—through the "lifeblood of [their] bitter pains," the kingdom of God may be built.

Following her Son to Golgotha and suffering with him in his agonizing work of redemption, Mary was "the archetype of followers of the cross for all time," who stood "by the side of the Redeemer."[39] Mary's love for her Son never wavered. Even a pierced heart could not destroy her love; perhaps, indeed, it intensified and expanded. Like Mary who battled against evil as "co-redeemer by the side of the Redeemer,"[40] all women are to be willing to join the fight for the kingdom. In accordance with the prophecy that women will do battle with the serpent:

> It has been woman's mission to war against evil and to educate her posterity to do the same; this has been true of woman including the Mother of the Son who conquered death and hell, but it will have to remain so until the end of the world.[41]

In coming to know Mary, Edith did not find a passive bystander but a strong, courageous woman who stood at the foot of her Son's cross. Edith understood that Mary's example and intercession help us to grow closer to God and neighbor, to give our own ready fiats, and to meet crises and challenges courageously. Marian devotion, then, has the power to impact personal lives and contemporary times; it always concerns practical reality.

When Edith became a cloistered nun, she grew all the more convinced that the spiritual weapons of prayer and sacrifice would win victory of good over evil. She was not blind or naïve to the possibility that the fruits of these good works might not appear in her lifetime. She wrote:

> Because hidden souls do not live in isolation, but are a part of the living nexus and have a position in a great divine order, we speak of an invisible Church. Their impact and affinity can remain hidden from themselves and others for their entire earthly lives. But it is also possible for some of this to become visible in the external world. This is how it was with the persons and events intertwined in the mystery of the Incarnation. Mary and Joseph, Zechariah and Elizabeth, the shepherds and the kings, Simeon and Anna—all of these had behind them a solitary life with God and were prepared for their special tasks before they found themselves together in those awesome encounters and events.[42]

From her hidden life behind the cloistered walls, Edith realized that God was preparing her, too, for a special task. She realized the urgency of her prayer and sacrifice for the darkened world. She forcefully urged her religious Sisters: "...the more an era is engulfed in the night of sin and estrangement from God, the more it needs souls united to God. And God does not permit a deficiency. The greatest figures of prophecy and sanctity step forth out of the darkest night."[43] These words betrayed Edith's grave concern; she wrote them from her convent in Echt, Holland, soon before the Nazis invaded that country.

Edith's Relationship with Mary

Some argue that Edith's relationship with the Blessed Mother was directly related to her strained relationship with her mother. Might Edith have turned to the comfort of the Blessed Mother because of Frau Stein's rejection of her conversion? This is unlikely. The inability of mother and daughter to share and practice the same faith caused them such pain precisely because they cared for each other so much.

Perhaps Edith's love and admiration for her mother enabled her to so readily turn to Mary. Edith admired the way her mother exercised a maternal compassion and influence on not only her biological children, but also her extended family, neighbors, employees, and even strangers. Edith likely saw in her mother the strong women so extolled in the Old Testament.

Frau Stein was a woman who knew how to fight for what she held dear. To Edith, she was a respected and beloved mother, protector, provider, and mentor. Perhaps in recognizing the similarities between Frau Stein and Mary, Edith could foster her Marian spirituality without diminishing her love for her mother.

When Edith delivered her address, "The Ethos of Women's Professions," she spoke with the passion of someone who had an authentic relationship with Mary. Her audiences seemed to recognize her authenticity, as

one person praised, "...her bearing when she descended
from the podium recalled those paintings in which
ancient masters depicted Mary's visit to the Temple."[44]
In fact, in her intense prayer life, she seemed to image
Mother Church. A Benedictine monk, Father Damasus
Zahringer, remembered the first time he saw Edith at
the Beuron Abbey. He noted:

> [H]er appearance and attitude made an impression on
> me that I can only compare with that of pictures of *eccle-*
> *sia orans* [the church praying] in the oldest ecclesiastical
> art of the catacombs. Apart from the arms uplifted in
> prayer, everything about her was reminiscent of that
> Christian archetype.... She was in truth a type of that
> *ecclesia*, standing in the world of time and yet apart from
> it, and knowing nothing else, in the depths of her union
> with Christ, but the Lord's words: "For them do I sancti-
> fy myself; that they also may be sanctified in the
> truth."[45]

Edith also demonstrated her Marian devotion by celebrating Marian feasts, praying the Rosary, and striving
to imitate Mary's virtues, particularly her humble obedience and maternal love. Humility was the cornerstone
of Edith's work and life. She knew that in order to carry
divine life into the world she first needed to put her life
into God's hands, and she strove to do this daily. As a
teacher, she proved herself a "loving educator for
Christ" as she impressed her students not only with her
intellectual life, but also with her obvious love of Christ
and of each of them.

In 1933, Edith brought her Marian spirituality,
pruned and shaped during her eleven years in the secular world, into the cloister. As she entered the Cologne
Carmel, Edith stood at the convent grille and was asked

to choose a hymn to sing. She did not hesitate in her selection, "Bless Us, Mary," but felt awkward about actually singing before an audience, even a small group of religious Sisters.[46] Shyly, she sang the hymn, later confessing that this was more difficult than giving a public lecture to a large audience.

Throughout her nine years as a Carmelite, Edith would continue to ask for Mary's blessing. Daily she strove to grow close to Mary, passionately praying for her maternal guidance and support, particularly in bringing peace to the world. Edith prayed and requested prayers for her family's safety and well-being. Frau Stein's health was deteriorating steadily. In 1936, doctors discovered an inoperable cancerous tumor in her stomach. The prognosis was disheartening. The more ill Frau Stein became, the more she missed Edith.[47] It pained Edith deeply to know that her mother felt forsaken by her youngest child. On the Feast of the Exaltation of the Cross, September 14, 1936, Edith renewed her vows, and suddenly sensed her mother's presence. Her mother died at precisely that time. Edith felt convinced that her mother would be her helper from heaven.

For years, Edith's sister Rosa had wanted to join Edith in becoming a Catholic and even in entering Carmel. She had found it impossible to do so, knowing the pain it would cause their mother. She sacrificed her desire while Frau Stein was alive. After her mother succumbed to cancer, Rosa began to study for Baptism, receiving instruction from Edith herself. At this time, Edith was recuperating in the hospital from a broken foot and hand, the result of a fall down the convent steps, and she could visit with Rosa daily and help prepare her for the sacraments.[48] On Christmas Eve, Edith attended the long-awaited and joyful celebrations of Rosa's Baptism and First Holy Communion. Capturing Rosa's joy, and perhaps her own memories of Baptism, Edith wrote a poignant poem, a gift to her sister:

> The secret of my heart, that for so long I had to hide,
> I now proclaim aloud
> I believe, I confess!...
> My heart has now become a crib
> That waits for you,
> Not for long!
> Mary, my Mother and your Mother,
> Has given me her name.
> At midnight she'll lay her newborn Child
> Into my heart.
> No human heart could ever conceive
> What you prepare for those who love you.[49]

Highlighting Mary's role in welcoming Rosa into the Church, and in carrying her Son's life into Rosa's heart, the poem conveys an appreciation of Mary as Mother of God and our Mother. It also expresses the joy and peace of a heart united to Christ, and it stands in stark contrast to the fear and chaos in the outside world.

In October 1937, the Cologne Carmelites marked their 300th year jubilee with a celebration that included a "principal guest of honor": a statue of the Queen of Peace from a nearby church in Schnurgasse.[50] Describing the jubilee ceremonies and the impressive public attendance, Edith hinted at the chaos outside the convent walls, writing, "One has to be grateful that something like this [celebration] is still possible."[51]

On Good Friday, 1938, months before Kristallnacht, Edith turned her attention from Advent expectation to

Lenten sacrifice in her Marian poem, "Standing with You Beneath the Cross." Even the poem's beginning is a powerful expression of Edith's love of Mary and the cross:

Today I stood with you beneath the cross,
And felt more clearly than I ever did
That you became our Mother only there.

Conveying her respect, gratitude, and love for Mary, Edith described the heavy cost of Mary's motherhood and discipleship:

...with the lifeblood of your bitter pains
You purchased life anew for every soul.

Mary's role as mother embraces us all:

You know us all, our wounds, our imperfections;
But you also know the celestial radiance
That your Son's love would shed on us in heaven.
Thus carefully you guide our faltering footsteps,
No price too high for you to lead us to our goal.

The concluding lines show a noticeable shift in emphasis, as Edith considered the "lifeblood" of our pain as we care for those souls God has entrusted to us:

...those whom you have chosen for companions
To stand with you around the eternal throne,
They here must stand with you beneath the cross,
And with the lifeblood of their own bitter pains
Must purchase heavenly glory for those souls
Whom God's own Son entrusted to their care.[52]

Journeying with Queen Esther and Mary to the Cross

Certainly, Edith never had been a stranger to "bitter pain," including the heartbreak of watching another suffer and being unable to help with any human means. The pain was greatest when she knew she was the cause of another's suffering, such as her dear mother's. Edith nevertheless remained convinced of the life-giving power of suffering.

Only months after Edith wrote her Marian poem, she would realize more fully the "bitter pains" of the world and the possible "lifeblood" of her own suffering. On November 9, 1938, German Jews were subjected to a night of horror in the infamous "night of broken glass," Kristallnacht. The violence continued through November 10. In her desire to bring light to a society submerged in darkness, Edith offered herself to God, and trusted that he had accepted her life for her family.[53] Remaining passionately focused on her vocation, she identified herself with Queen Esther "who was taken from among her people precisely that she might represent them before the king."[54]

Edith would continue to hold the image of Esther close to her heart as she moved to Holland, a step taken in obedience to her superiors. She asked for one favor: to make a slight detour to a Carmelite church in Schnurgasse to pray before a statue of the Queen of Peace, the same statue that had been present at the convent's jubilee celebration the year before. After praying there, Sister Teresa Benedicta of the Cross continued her journey to Holland. There, she found security, but, as she had anticipated, it was short-lived.

During this time, Edith's love of Christ and his Mother continued to deepen. She surrendered to Christ, understanding that "…nothing can give [Mary's] most pure heart greater joy than an ever deeper surrender to the Divine Heart."[55] During Lent 1940, immediately prior to the Nazi invasion of Holland, she was asked to compose a Mass and Litany in honor of the Blessed Virgin Mary, *Regina Pacis* [Queen of Peace], for the Cologne Carmelites. Considering it a privilege, Edith finished this work, explaining that the Carmelites would be petitioning Rome "for a first class feast, preferably for the whole Church" in honor of the Queen of Peace.[56]

Edith's prayers for peace intensified when the Nazis invaded Holland in May 1940. Her essays and letters, her demeanor and expressions indicated an ever-deepening prayer life and a heightened awareness of the chaos and terror in the world. Her prayer life did not insulate her from the world, but rather encouraged her to journey closer to the cross. She would keep her eyes focused on the crucified Christ and his Sorrowful Mother, and she would not lose hope.

On the Feast of the Exaltation of the Cross in 1941, Edith wrote:

> The love of Christ impels [us] to descend into the darkest night. And no earthly maternal joy resembles the bliss of a soul permitted to enkindle the light of grace in the night of sins. The way to this is the cross. Beneath the cross the Virgin of virgins becomes the Mother of Grace.[57]

Close to Mary, Edith knew that we may experience the sorrow of a broken heart, but also the joy of collaborating with God to mend a broken world.

In June 1941, Edith wrote a fictional dialogue with Queen Esther as the main character. Because Edith considered herself a "poor little Esther," the dialogue may be seen as a veiled autobiography and perhaps a foreshadowing of Edith's suffering at the hands of the Nazis. The fictional conversation is between Queen Esther and Mother Antonia (Edith's prioress). Esther first is presented as a stranger at the door, and then as a Marian figure whose prayer and sacrifice helped to save the Jewish people. In this dialogue, Edith displayed her creative talent and her insightful assessment of the plight of the Jewish people of her day as well as her spiritual plan to help them and the world situation. She wrote the following words, indicating Mother Antonia's response to a stranger's search for lodgings:

> *Mother:*
> Looking for lodgings? How the word touches me!
> I am reminded of that pure one, the Immaculate,
> Who once about this time also sought lodgings.
> *(Kneels down):*
> Oh, tell me! Are you she herself, the Virgin Mother?
>
> *Stranger (raises her up):*
> I am not she—but I know her very well,
> And it is my joy to serve her,
> I am of her people, her blood.
> And once I risked my life for this people.
> You recall her when you hear my name.
> My life serves as [an] image of hers for you.[58]

Esther then explains what she did for the Jewish people, concluding:

> This is how the highest Lord freed his people
> Through Esther, his maidservant, from the hands of Haman.

Mother Antonia responds perceptively:

> And today another Haman
> Has sworn to annihilate them in bitter hate.[59]

Edith's fictional dialogue vividly reminded the Sisters of the hatred outside the convent walls and the loving prayers and sacrifice needed to overcome it. It confirmed Edith's commitment to sacrifice as expressed only months after she entered Carmel when she wrote: "All one can do is try to live the life one has chosen with ever greater fidelity and purity in order to offer it up as an acceptable sacrifice for all one is connected with."[60]

By the end of 1941, in addition to her letters and essays, Edith was busy researching a major study of John of the Cross, titled "Science of the Cross." As she immersed herself in reading about the saint, she critically assessed a biographer: "He is completely silent about the apparitions of the Mother of God."[61] Writing her own book on St. John, she would not neglect his Marian spirituality. In fact, she referred to Mary immediately in the introduction, noting how Mary rescued the young John twice from drowning. Edith also emphasized the role of John's mother in fostering within him a love of Mary, explaining that

> ...when the young widow who bore such want and suffering spoke to her children about their Mother in heaven she surely also led them to know Mary as the Mother of Sorrows beside the cross. And in all reverence for the mysteries regarding the guiding influence of grace, we may surely suppose that Mary herself would have taught her protégé the science of the cross in good time. Who could be as well instructed in it and as well penetrated by its value as the wisest of virgins?[62]

Perhaps Edith's words betray her own gratitude to Mary for her maternal guidance; perhaps she realized that she, too, was a "protégé" of Mary, being taught the "science of the cross in good time." That time reached its fullness on August 2, 1942, when the Nazis arrested Sister Teresa Benedicta of the Cross, imprisoning her in a transit camp before sending her to her death in Auschwitz. How did Edith conduct herself as she entered the first camp? The question calls to mind Edith's demeanor when she first embarked on her lecturing career and a witness noticed how her descent from the podium "recalled those paintings in which ancient masters depicted Mary's visit to the Temple." One wonders about Edith's descent from the cattle car into a Nazi camp. Could it have been similar to Mary's demeanor as she ascended to Golgotha?

In the midst of the world's terror, Edith lived her life to help others, and, more than that, she was willing to give her life for others with the "lifeblood of... [her] own bitter pains." She continued to imitate Mary's strength, and, like Mary, she kept her focus on Christ. Was it Mary's intercession that helped her to see that the "dear child Jesus is with us even here"? Indeed, as she headed to her death in Auschwitz, she so mirrored Mary's courage and sorrow that one witness referred to her as the Pietá.

The student of the science of the cross had been mentored well; now the student imaged the teacher. Relying on the grace of God, Sister Teresa Benedicta of the Cross stood firm, as the Sorrowful Mother did, remaining faithful to her vocation, her heart open to "those souls whom God's own Son entrusted to her care."

It is only after we surrender ourselves completely to God's will, as Mary did, that we can rejoice like Mary, "singing the jubilant song of the holy Virgin, 'My soul proclaims the greatness of the Lord, and my spirit rejoices in God my Savior. For he has done great things for me, and holy is his name.'"[63]

CHAPTER 5

Carrying the Cross into a World in Flames

Never immune from life's painful experiences and challenging burdens, Edith slowly learned that the mystery of suffering is linked to the mystery of love. Edith came to know that when two mysteries are connected, they become no less mysterious. Their meanings are not to be discovered as if they are problems to be solved, riddles to be deciphered, or puzzles to be completed. They are not mere guessing games; rather, they often leave us unable to speak and unable to see. This is because mysteries speak the language of silence and paint the picture of darkness. So, too, in the spiritual life, the mysteries of suffering and love call for a faith journey born of silence and transformed by darkness.

From that silence and darkness, God brings his word and light. Edith explained:

> To erect the structure of holiness...one must dig deep and build high, must descend into the depths of the dark night of one's own nothingness in order to be

raised up high into the sunlight of divine love and compassion.[1]

Confronted by suffering in the world and experiencing no small degree of personal pain and hardship, Edith never sank into self-pity. Even if she may have pondered why evil was becoming so powerful, she converted the "whys" of suffering into wise suffering by asking a self-reflective "how." How could she help alleviate another's suffering? How could she collaborate with God in his work of redemption? She found that words paled in comparison to an image: the face of the Son of God, Love himself, scourged and crucified for love. "Naked and exposed, the Lord hung on the cross." In his suffering, love prevailed as the drama of redemption unfolded.[2] The drama is a story of love betrayed in the Garden of Eden and tested in the Garden of Gethsemane. It is a love fulfilled on Golgotha near another garden. From the tomb in that garden, Love rose gloriously on Easter morning.

Edith came to understand that for Christians who allow love to enter the picture of human suffering, the image of the face of the suffering Christ comes alive. A superficial, passing glance at this image will not suffice, but only a long, penetrating gaze into the eyes of the One who loves eternally. The love story begins with this gaze, but does not end there; it continues with a response of love returned. This is why Edith pleaded with her fellow Sisters to look at the crucifix and gaze at the Crucified who spilled his blood for each of us. She wrote:

> The Savior hangs before you with a pierced heart. He has spilled his heart's blood to win your heart. If you

want to follow him in holy *purity*, your heart must be free of every earthly desire. Jesus, the Crucified, is to be the only object of your longings, your wishes, your thoughts.... The arms of the Crucified are spread out to draw you to his heart. He wants your life in order to give you his.³

Edith knew that it is not enough simply to know of Christ and his passion. It is not even enough to follow his teaching. Christ invites us into his friendship. A friend will respond with love. Desiring the good of the Beloved, this love seeks to faithfully imitate him— indeed, to be an image of him, even in his suffering, and to reflect his goodness to suffering humanity. Having embraced suffering and the sufferer, this love fervently hopes to enter into the joy of paradise and to stand before the Beloved, seeing him in radiant glory.

For Edith the life and spirituality of John of the Cross powerfully illustrate such a love story, one that encourages us to keep our focus on the cross. She explained:

It is beneficial to honor the Crucified in images and to fashion such as will encourage devotion to him. But better than any image made of wood or stone are living images. To form souls to the image of Christ, to plant the cross in their hearts, this was the great task in the life of [John of the Cross].... All of his writings are in the service of this task. His letters and the testimonials to his activities speak even more personally of his dedication.⁴

Edith's vocation, like that of St. John, was "to form souls to the image of Christ, to plant the cross in their hearts...." And, similar to St. John, her letters and essays were "in the service of that task." Her words and actions consistently reflected her love of the suffering Savior and her embrace of his cross.

How did Edith come to understand the hidden meaning of the cross? Certainly she drew from a variety of sources and lessons: the witness and testimony of the grieving widow, Edith's own prayer life, her relationship with the Sorrowful Mother, her recourse to the sacraments, and her participation in the liturgy of the Eucharist. She also grew in her understanding of the cross as she immersed herself in the Lenten season, spending time in silence in the Benedictine Abbey in Beuron, intensifying her prayer life, and pondering the passion of Christ. More than pondering the passion, she seemed to be entering into it. She once explained, "For every year on Palm Sunday and in the Sacred Triduum the liturgy of the Church presents the final days in Jesus' life, his death, and his resting in the tomb to the faithful with dramatic vigor, in moving words, melodies, and ceremonies that inexorably compel one to share the experience."[5] Her words seem to reflect her own experience.

Edith's journey to the cross was particularly directed by her ongoing study and deepening love of Scripture. She understood that Scripture was the key to St. John's deep insights into the mystery of the cross. Edith explained:

> We can count on it, then, that the message of the cross contained in the divine Word had an ever new effect on his heart throughout his life. It is utterly impossible to treat this perhaps most important source of his science of the cross exhaustively. For we must assert from the start that the *entire* sacred Scripture—the Old as well as the New Testament—was his daily bread.[6]

Edith, too, devoured Scripture as her daily bread, and learned the message of the Cross. From the Old

Testament, she pondered the role of Queen Esther and the sacrifice of Abraham. Having been born on the Day of Atonement, she particularly considered passages related to this feast as she came to grasp that it was "the Old Testament antecedent of Good Friday."[7] From the New Testament, Edith immersed herself in the passion of Christ, even coming to recognize that Christ's cross was present not only as he prepared for his crucifixion, but also when he first entered the world through Mary.

Pondering Christ's life, death, and resurrection, Edith considered the meaning of his suffering and his response to the pain and humanity's struggles. She appreciated that he who came to love and to give abundant love was dealt abundant suffering. He was moved with compassion, even as he was persecuted. His heart never grew cold, even as he journeyed toward the cross. His heart continued to burn with love as he encountered and responded to the pained pleas of the sick and afflicted. He suffered. He loved. He suffered because he loved.

Demonstrating his love by absolute obedience and self-surrender, Jesus sought to do his Father's will, praying an agonizing, heart-wrenching plea in the Garden of Gethsemane. Edith pondered Christ's prayer:

> By his hour on the Mount of Olives, he prepared himself for his road to Golgotha. A few short words tell us what he implored of his Father during this most difficult hour of his life, words that are given to us as guiding stars for our own hours on the Mount of Olives. "Father, if you are willing, take this cup away from me. Nevertheless, let your will be done, not mine." Like lightning, these words for an instant illumine for us the innermost spiritual life of Jesus, the unfathomable mystery of his God-man existence and his dialogue with the Father.[8]

In our own "hours on the Mount of Olives," how do we unite our wills with the Father's will? Love is the key. Like a magnet, it draws Christians to the cross. It is the catalyst that propels them from the cross to daily life where Christ's love continues to touch and animate their souls. Edith contemplated Mark's Gospel and Jesus' invitation: "If anyone wishes to be my disciple let him deny himself, take up his cross, and follow me. For whoever would save his life will lose it, but whoever loses it for my sake will save it" (Mk 8:34–35ff.). She realized that the way of the cross demands self-denial and self-sacrifice. "The more perfect this active and passive crucifixion may be, the more intimate will be the union with the crucified and therefore the richer the participation in the divine life." [9]

The Christian vocation, then, does not guarantee a pain-free existence, for it calls the soul closer to the cross. When the soul responds to the invitation to intimacy, it is not a superficial act of piety that permits comfortable living but rather self-sacrificial giving. Edith understood that even small sacrifices have the potential for great good, as she emphasized:

> This is the "little way," a bouquet of insignificant little blossoms that are daily placed before the Almighty—perhaps a silent, lifelong martyrdom that no one suspects and that is at the same time a source of deep peace and hearty joyousness and a fountain of grace that bubbles over everything—we do not know where it goes, and the people whom it reaches do not know from whence it comes. [10]

Edith gave many examples from the school of Christian suffering, including the struggles of Teresa of

Avila, John of the Cross, and Monica. In a fictional dialogue between Ambrose and Augustine, Edith captured Monica's dual suffering due to and on behalf of her son. Edith wrote of Ambrose's praise of Monica:

> O Augustine, thank God for your mother.
> She is your angel before the eternal throne;
> Her commerce is in heaven, and her petitions
> Fall, like steady drops, heavily into the bowl
> Of compassion...
> Therefore, she now weeps sweet tears of joy,
> And she is richly rewarded for all her suffering.[11]

Monica's suffering was like "commerce" in heaven, fruitful because of her collaboration with God's work of love. Edith understood that suffering has the limitless capacity of igniting and sustaining love in those who suffer as well in all those associated with them. The more we progress in our spiritual journey, drawing closer to the heart of Christ, the more we recognize love's role in suffering. Edith's poetry and letters suggest the importance of examining the way we suffer. Do we suffer with love, that is, in a loving way? Do we strive to be united to God in our suffering so that God's life and love may empower all our crosses? Are we willing to suffer for love, that is, for that which we hold dear and for all those whom we hold dear? Have we broadened the scope of "loved ones" in our lives? Are we willing to suffer for Love—for God and for God's kingdom?

Suffering with love implies both an attitude and a relationship, for the sufferer seeks to have both a disposition of love and a relationship with God, who is Love. The attitude and relationship are inherent in Christ's command to take up his cross (see Lk 9:23). His statement is not so much an omen of future suffering as a divine promise that he will accompany those who carry their crosses and follow him.

God's grace supports, consoles, and strengthens us, teaching the meaning of generous, self-giving love, a love that may encourage us to lay down our lives for a friend. Edith explained, "Our goal is union with God, our way that of the crucified Christ, our becoming one with him takes place when we are crucified."[12] Suffering with love, then, focuses the attention away from self and onto Christ, unshackling the fetters of self-pity and unleashing the powers of self-giving. It implies solidarity with all those who suffer.

The sacramental life of the Church affirms the solidarity of love among her members. Particularly in the Eucharist, we are drawn into the love of Christ, and consequently from his love out to suffering humanity. "...[W]e are made members of the Body of Christ by virtue of the sacrament in which Christ himself is present. When we partake of the sacrifice and receive Holy Communion and are nourished by the flesh and blood of Jesus, we ourselves become his flesh and his blood."[13] Living Eucharistic lives, we are strengthened in our ministry of love by Love himself.

The Divine Physician who strengthens us also purifies us, sometimes giving us medicine that does not necessarily alleviate pain. Indeed, sometimes it is tough-love medicine that hurts as it perfects. Edith knew that "...no spiritual work comes into the world without severe labor pains."[14] While growth pains principally imply suffering for one's own sanctification, labor pains principally imply suffering for the sanctification of others.

Edith understood that when love enters suffering, it is an animating force, truly capable of giving life to the soul, and to those souls with whom it comes into contact. Indeed, suffering can give birth to love. Entering into the heart of the mystery of suffering is not a solitary endeavor; the Divine Teacher accompanies individuals on their journey, and he takes the lead. Christ and his followers shoulder the cross together, and only then does the burden become light. Even Christ was not alone on his road to Calvary:

> Not only are there adversaries around him who oppress him, but also people who succor him.... Everyone who, in the course of time, has borne an onerous destiny in remembrance of the suffering Savior or who has freely taken up works of expiation has by doing so canceled some of the mighty load of human sin and has helped the Lord carry his burden. Or rather, Christ the head effects expiation in these members of his Mystical Body who put themselves, body and soul, at his disposal for carrying out his work of salvation.[15]

True labors of love are not divorced from joy or hope, just as a woman's labor pains are preceded by and mingled with tears of happiness. Edith understood and accepted that the task of carrying divine life into the world would entail some measure of suffering, but she trusted that the task would bear fruit with the help of the crucified Redeemer.

Edith stressed that some individuals may falsely think that they are called to suffer, but this may be dangerous without consultation with a spiritual director. It also could be dangerous if the desire is divorced from love. Without love, a desire to suffer is perverse and poisonous; it cannot bear fruit.

Wary of those who may have had such a perverted desire, Edith stressed that a true vocation to suffer comes from God, who is inviting the soul to union with him. The closer the soul journeys to the heart of Christ, the more it may be asked to suffer for the good of another. This is God's invitation, and therefore can only be undertaken when his voice is clearly discerned. Edith wrote:

> When someone desires to suffer, it is not merely a pious reminder of the suffering of the Lord. Voluntary expiatory suffering is what truly and really unites one to the Lord intimately. When it arises, it comes from an already existing relationship with Christ.... Only someone whose spiritual eyes have been opened to the supernatural correlations of worldly events can desire suffering in expiation, and this is only possible for people in whom the spirit of Christ dwells.[16]

Thus, it is a special person who is asked to take up such a cross, the person who has been invited by Christ into a unique relationship with him. It is a person who has grown tremendously along the spiritual journey and whose life is surrendered to God and animated by his Spirit.

The vocation to suffer in expiation, then, is embraced faithfully by those who already have a deeply intimate relationship with the crucified Savior. Edith explained to a friend:

> There is a vocation to suffer with Christ and thereby to cooperate with him in his work of salvation. When we are united with the Lord, we are members of the Mystical Body of Christ: Christ lives on in his members and continues to suffer in them. And the suffering borne in union with the Lord is his suffering, incorpo-

rated in the great work of salvation and fruitful there-in.[17]

With profound understanding, Edith appreciated the spiritual dimensions of the suffering of the great saints and martyrs of the Church, and she, too, was willing to lay down her life for God. She was well acquainted with the great Carmelite saints, John of the Cross and Teresa of Avila. She knew from their teaching that not all people are called to heroic martyrdom. Edith, though, was convinced that she had such a calling. She consulted with her spiritual directors and religious superiors as she drew closer to Christ's cross. She was so connected to God's love and immersed in that love that she was willing to risk suffering, even physical death, in order to collaborate with God in the work of his kingdom. After much prayerful consideration and guidance, Edith realized that God was calling her to suffer for the good of the world.

Edith's Embrace of the Cross

Seeking to follow Christ, imitate him, resemble him, and grow in intimacy with him, Edith anticipated that she could not experience the depths of love without some measure of suffering. She seemed to understand that her life would continue to be a love story with each chapter testifying to love's splendor, but also to its pain. Each chapter would not close the story, but would build on the lessons of love. As an image of Christ's love, nothing superficial or shallow would taint it, for it was the image of the perfect love of Christ. It would shine forth only after it was purified; it would soar to the heights only after it plummeted to the depths. Edith's ascent in love enabled her to reach out to suffering humanity. Such sympathetic concern seemed to grow in proportion to her embrace of the cross.

When she first was introduced to the mystery of the cross in 1917, Edith found that her "unbelief shattered" as she converted to Christianity. Now, with another World War and her radical embrace of the cross, Edith's concern for the Jewish people only intensified. Her conversion did not detract from her love for her own people. By 1933, Edith realized her concerns were well founded as she received credible reports about their plight. One evening, while living with the Notre Dame Sisters at the Collegium Marianum in Münster, Edith was somehow locked out of her dormitory. A Catholic couple noticed Edith's vain attempts to open the door and invited her into their home for the night. While they prepared Edith's room, her hosts noted that American newspapers were reporting on the cruelty the Nazis were inflicting on the Jewish people. Edith did not reveal her Jewish ancestry for fear of disturbing "their night's rest by such a revelation." Their words confirmed what Edith already had heard, but "now," Edith explained, "it dawned on me that once again God had put a heavy hand upon his people, and that the fate of this people would also be mine."[18] She was certain that she would share in the suffering of her Jewish brothers and sisters. The thought plagued her mind and heart as concern for their welfare escalated.

In 1933, Edith intended to spend time during Lent at the Benedictine Abbey of Beuron, a place she often retreated to for silence, solitude, and communal prayer.

But the purpose for her visit was different: "This time a special reason drew me there. During the past weeks I had constantly given thought to whether I could do something about the plight of the Jews. Finally I had made a plan to travel to Rome and to ask the Holy Father in a private audience for an encyclical."[19] She would need to consult with her spiritual director and obtain his permission to meet with Pope Pius XI.

What prompted Edith to think that she would be granted a private audience with the Pope? Certainly it did not stem from an over-inflated ego but, rather, a humble recognition that her name and work were well-known in Catholic circles, even in the Vatican, and from her sense of responsibility as a Catholic woman of Jewish descent. She felt called to step forward and speak up forcefully. She had given many speeches about the vocation of women to exert a maternal presence in the world and to fight for the kingdom of God. She had written many essays on the importance of taking up the cross. Her words would come alive in the dark night of Nazi oppression.

Before going on retreat, she met with her friend Hedwig Spiegel, who was preparing for Baptism. On Good Friday, Edith and Hedwig attended services of the passion of the Lord at the Carmelite chapel of Cologne. Edith's prayer during the services empowered her to embrace the cross in a radical way:

> He [the priest] spoke beautifully and movingly, but something other than his words occupied me more intensely. I talked with the Savior and told him that I knew that it was his cross that was now being placed upon the Jewish people; that most of them did not

understand this; but that those who did, would have to take it up willingly in the name of all. I would do that. He should only show me how. At the end of the service, I was certain that I had been heard. But what this carrying of the cross was to consist in, that I did not yet know.[20]

When Edith met with her spiritual director, she learned that a private audience with the Pope would be impossible, for tremendous crowds were flooding into Rome to celebrate the nineteenth centennial of the death of Christ. According to Edith, "At best I might be admitted to a 'semiprivate' audience," i.e., an audience in a small group. "That did not serve my purpose."[21]

She came up with a new plan. She would write a letter to the Pope, to be hand-delivered by her spiritual director. On April 12, Edith began her letter with these words:

As a child of the Jewish people who, by the grace of God, for the past eleven years has also been a child of the Catholic Church, I dare to speak to the Father of Christendom that which oppresses millions of Germans. For weeks we have seen deeds perpetrated in Germany that mock any sense of justice and humanity, not to mention love of neighbor.

She wrote directly from the heart, as she pleaded with the Pope:

For weeks not only Jews but also thousands of faithful Catholics in Germany, and, I believe, all over the world, have been waiting and hoping for the Church of Christ to raise its voice to put a stop to this abuse of Christ's name. Is not this idolization of race and governmental power that is being pounded into the public consciousness by the radio open heresy? Isn't the effort to destroy Jewish blood an abuse of the holiest humanity of our Savior, of the most blessed Virgin and the apostles?[22]

The letter was hand-delivered, but Edith never received a response other than a papal blessing for her and her family.[23]

Edith's time in the outside world was drawing to a close as she prepared to enter Carmel. Her brother-in-law Hans Biberstein accused her of distancing herself from the Jewish people:

> What I was planning appeared to him to draw the line between myself and the Jewish people more sharply than before, and that just now when they were so sorely oppressed. The fact that I saw it very differently, he could not understand.[24]

In joining Carmel, Edith was not running *away*, but running *to*; she was not escaping, but embracing. She desired to fully embrace the cross, as she surrendered her life to Christ. In doing so, she believed she was drawing closer to the world, committing herself to prayer and sacrifice for suffering humanity. During the eleven years between her Baptism and her entrance into Carmel, Edith had solidified her understanding of the redemptive suffering she would come to know, particularly as a Carmelite nun. She explained that the "fundamental premise of all religious life, above all of the life of Carmel, [is] to stand proxy for sinners through voluntary and joyous suffering, and to cooperate in the salvation of humankind."[25]

Edith chose a religious name that was a beautiful witness to her vocation: Sister Teresa Benedicta of the

Cross. Certainly, the name reflected her love of St. Teresa of Avila, who inspired her conversion, and it reflected her love of the Benedictines, having spent so much time in prayer at the Benedictine Abbey of Beuron and received spiritual direction from the Benedictine Archabbot Raphael Walzer. The word "cross" was an integral part of her life; indeed, it not only described her vocation, it also defined it. She was living a relationship with Christ crucified, fully embracing his cross:

> I received [my name] exactly as I requested it. By the cross I understood the destiny of God's people which, even at that time, began to announce itself. I thought that those who recognized it as the cross of Christ had to take it upon themselves in the name of all.[26]

As Edith grew in her relationship with Christ, she carried the cross closely and courageously. Remaining attuned to world events, she renewed her commitment to redemptive suffering. Edith's letters often reflected anguished concern that her family would fall victim to Nazi persecution. She suffered emotionally from knowing of the cruelty in the world and the dangers that threatened her friends and family. Some of them had already been imprisoned and forced into slave labor.

Recognizing the need of "the saving power of joyfully borne suffering," Edith was willing to suffer for the good of the world.[27] Edith's joy in suffering is incomprehensible unless seen in the light of love. She rejoiced that in her vocation she had the opportunity to imitate Christ and share in his sufferings. She rejoiced, too, that in her suffering she might help to bring souls closer to God.

The closer she came to God, the more she came to feel responsible for building his kingdom. She urged her fellow Sisters, "In our time, when the powerlessness of all natural means for battling the overwhelming misery everywhere has been demonstrated so obviously, an entirely new understanding of the power of prayer, of expiation, and of vicarious atonement has again awakened."[28] It was reawakened in Edith herself: "Certainly, today I know more of what it means to be wedded to the Lord in the sign of the cross. Of course, one can never comprehend it, for it is a mystery."[29]

A few months following Kristallnacht, after Edith had settled into her new home at the convent of Echt, Holland, she had a foreboding that it was "the twelfth hour."

On Passion Sunday, March 26, 1939, she asked permission of her prioress to offer herself "to the heart of Jesus as a sacrifice of propitiation for true peace, that the dominion of the Antichrist may collapse, if possible, without a new world war...." In humility she acknowledged: "I am nothing, but Jesus desires it, and surely he will call many others to do likewise in these days."[30]

These words, including her inspiring essays to her Carmelite Sisters, took on a tone of urgency. She considered how the cross was being desecrated in the world. "More than ever the cross is a sign of contradiction. The followers of the Antichrist show it far more dishonor than did the Persians who stole it.[31] They desecrate the images of the cross, and they make every effort to tear the cross out of the hearts of Christians."[32] Against these actions, the Sisters needed to respond to the Savior's gaze:

...the Savior today looks at us, solemnly probing us, and asks each one of us: Will you remain faithful to the Crucified? Consider carefully! The world is in flames, the battle between Christ and the Antichrist has broken into the open. If you decide for Christ, it could cost you your life.[33]

Her warning to the Sisters grew more urgent:

The conflagration can also reach our house. But high above all flames towers the cross. They cannot consume it. It is the path from earth to heaven.... Look at the cross. From the open heart gushes the blood of the Savior. This extinguishes the flames of hell.[34]

Approximately a year later Edith's prediction became even more pressing as the war came closer to the convent's door. In May 1940, the Nazis invaded Holland.

Soon after the occupation, the Nazis searched the residence of the Most Reverend Jozef Lemmens, Bishop of Roermond. The bishop stood firm, defiantly predicting their defeat and God's victory over the evils they perpetrated. He later visited Sister Teresa Benedicta of the Cross, her sister Rosa (now a Third Order Carmelite), and the other Carmelite Sisters. Bishop Lemmens advised them of the political climate and encouraged them to be steadfast in their vocations and tireless in their prayer and sacrifice. They must be committed to the truth no matter what the repercussions. Bishop Lemmens showed fatherly concern to Edith and Rosa, and he suggested that they move out of the country. Edith and Rosa adamantly stated that they would stay. Their response likely edified Bishop Lemmens, and in turn his courage edified and inspired Edith, especially his willingness to be a martyr for Christ.[35]

Edith's spiritual essays during the occupation reflect heartfelt concern for those outside the cloister. She wrote fervent and passionate words as she urged her Sisters to deeper prayer and sacrifice:

> Today we live again in a time that urgently needs to be renewed at the hidden springs of God-fearing souls. Many people, too, place their last hope in these hidden springs of salvation. This is a serious warning cry: Surrender without reservation to the Lord who has called us.[36]

Edith understood that people were relying on the Sisters' prayers, and the Sisters, therefore, needed to take their vocations all the more seriously. Prayer and sacrifice could transform the world. In surrendering to God

> the face of the earth may be renewed. In faithful trust, we must abandon our souls to the sovereignty of the Holy Spirit. It is not necessary that we experience the epiphany in our lives. We may live in confident certainty that what the Spirit of God secretly effects in us bears its fruits in the kingdom of God. We will see them in eternity.[37]

Edith further reflected:

> Just as the Lamb had to be killed to be raised upon the throne of glory, so the path to glory leads through suffering and the cross for everyone chosen to attend the marriage supper of the Lamb. All who want to be married to the Lamb must allow themselves to be fastened to the cross with him.[38]

On November 7, 1940, Edith was given the opportunity to delve deeper into the mystery of the cross. She remarked good-naturedly to a friend that her superior had asked her to do some research and writing.

Just now I am gathering material for a new work since our Reverend Mother wishes me to do some scholarly work again, as far as this will be possible in our living situation and under the present circumstances. I am very grateful to be allowed once more to do something before my brain rusts completely.[39]

The project, a study of John of the Cross, engaged her mind as well as her heart. It reflected scholarly research, clarity of thought, and the depths of her heartfelt concerns. It also reflected her own love of the crucified Savior, her embrace of the cross, and her courage in following him. She would study the science of the cross, even as she witnessed as an expert on the mystery of the cross; she would write about it, even as she lived it.

She explained her deepening understanding of the cross: "A *scientia cruces* [science of the cross] can be gained only when one comes to feel the cross radically."[40] As she studied major biographies of John of the Cross, she confessed: "I live almost constantly immersed in thoughts about our Holy Father John. That is a great grace."[41] The research and writing were not easy, however:

I have to produce everything with a great deal of effort. To be sure, the building plan is another gift bestowed on me, i.e., it unfolds little by little, but I have to quarry the stones by myself, and prepare them, and drag them into place.[42]

It would seem that early in Edith's Christian journey, she was introduced to the *mystery* of the cross by the widow Anna Reinach; now Edith was introduced to the *science* of the cross by John of the Cross. For Edith, the image of Anna Reinach presented a clue to the mystery of the meaning of the cross and a relationship with the crucified Savior. John of the Cross illuminated this meaning by drawing from the depths of his own experience of the cross. Edith understood "science" as not merely a

> theory, that is, with a body of...true propositions.... We are dealing with a well-recognized truth—a theology of the cross—but a living, real, and effective truth. It is buried in the soul like a seed that takes root there and grows.... From this living form and strength in one's innermost depths, a perspective of life arises, the image one has of God and of the world, and therefore one can find expression for it in a mode of thinking....[43]

As Edith headed into the final stages of her life, she came to know from John of the Cross:

> If the soul wishes to share [Christ's] life, she must pass though the death on the cross with him: like him, she must crucify her own nature through a life of mortification and self-denial and surrender herself to be crucified in suffering and death, as God may ordain or permit it. The more perfect this active and passive crucifixion may be, the more intimate will be the union with the Crucified and therefore the richer the participation in the divine life.[44]

She knew that her own suffering would draw her ever more deeply into divine life. Indeed, this was her vocation, a vocation to suffer, and she embraced it wholeheartedly and fearlessly.

After Edith and all non-Aryan Germans were declared "stateless" in the Netherlands, in December 1941, Edith was required to report to Gestapo offices for registration purposes. She did not greet the officers with the mandatory "Heil Hitler." She would not use her hands, consistently clasped in prayer or outstretched in self-surrender, to praise Hitler. Instead, this petite Carmelite nun looked at the Gestapo officer and said, "Praised be Jesus Christ." She later remarked that it might not have been the most prudent action, but she had been struck by the reality of the "battle between Christ and Lucifer."[45]

From behind cloistered walls, Edith spoke of "the sight of the world in which we live, the need and misery, and the abyss of human malice."[46] Perhaps it was because she was behind the cloistered walls that she understood powerfully the needs of the world. Perhaps her ever-deepening relationship with Christ enabled her to truly see what others could not: In this battle, good and evil were confronting each other; and the way to victory was through the cross and through those prayerful souls who silently and courageously carry the cross. "The world," she said, "is still deluged by mire.... The battle between Christ and the Antichrist is not yet over. The followers of Christ have their place in this battle, and their chief weapon is the cross."[47] Sister Teresa Benedicta of the Cross would not flee that battle; indeed, she found herself drawn more deeply into it. Her eyes would remain on the cross of Christ, and her commitment to the world would remain the same: to carry divine life wherever she would go, even to a Nazi concentration camp.

In the months following her encounter with the Gestapo, Edith appraised the perilous circumstances confronting her but remained calm as she continued to put her life in God's hands. By the summer of 1942, the deportation of Dutch Jews increased dramatically. Soon

Bishop Lemmens, whom Edith admired so much for his willingness to be both bishop and martyr, would unwittingly play a role in Edith's martyrdom. In July 1942, representatives of Protestant and Catholic churches, including Bishop Lemmens, sent a joint telegram of protest to Nazi officials, imploring them to cease their anti-Semitic measures. The Nazis promised that they would leave baptized Jews alone, but threatened retaliation should the letter of protest be read publicly. The Dutch Catholic bishops disregarded the Nazis' threat, and the letter was read from pulpits across Holland the following Sunday. Infuriated by the Catholic Church's defiant stance, the Nazis ordered the immediate arrest and deportation of Dutch Catholics of Jewish descent. They would make no exceptions.[48]

During this time, Edith was concluding her work on the science of the cross. It seemed that as Teresa of Avila had prepared Edith for the beginning of her Christian journey, John of the Cross was preparing her for her final journey.

On August 2, 1942, Sister Teresa Benedicta of the Cross was praying before the Blessed Sacrament when a knock sounded at the convent door. It had been less than a year since Edith had written the fictional dialogue between her prioress and Queen Esther, describing Esther's arrival at the convent. In the dialogue, Mother Antonia concluded, "And today another Haman has sworn to annihilate [the Jewish people] in bitter hate." Now, that hatred had come directly to the convent door.

Officers of the SS arrested Edith and Rosa, and gave them five minutes to pack and leave the convent. Edith's manuscript, *The Science of the Cross,* lay open in her room. Edith's words of a year before seemed to be fulfilled: "If we [have been] faithful and are then driven out into the street, the Lord will send his angels to encamp themselves around us, and their invisible pinions will enclose our souls more securely than the highest and strongest walls."[49]

Edith was literally "driven out into the street." It was the day after the Feast of St. Peter in Chains, a feast to which Edith was particularly drawn "as a commemoration of being freed from fetters through the ministry of the angels."[50] As the Nazis drove Edith and Rosa to an internment camp, they lost their way and wandered aimlessly well into the night. Edith's essay, written only months before, seemed eerily prophetic. She had written of the infant Christ having "no place to lay his head," and concluded: "Whoever follows him must know that we have no lasting dwelling here.... God did not pledge to leave us within the walls of the enclosure forever. He need not do so because he has other walls to protect us."[51]

Edith knew the real meaning of freedom, one the world could never give, the freedom that came from uniting her will to God's. Two years before her arrest, Edith explained:

> Holy obedience binds our feet so that they no longer go their own way, but God's way. Children of the world say they are free when they are not subject to another's will.... The children of God see freedom as something else. They want to be unhindered in following the Spirit of God.[52]

The Nazis took the Steins to two internment camps, worlds of terror and uncertainty, where some inmates sobbed and others were paralyzed in fear. Edith did not seem to suffer in the same way. She had prepared herself for the possibility of great suffering and, more accurately, she was convinced that God had prepared her for this day. She was serene, yet profoundly sorrowful. She knew that members of her immediate family had been imprisoned in concentration camps, and now she knew how much they must be suffering. She also now grasped, in horror, the depth of the torment of the Jewish people. She wanted to help in her own unique way: by praying, whispering words of comfort, and even smiling. In her Carmelite habit she projected the reality of eternal life with God, and by her serene demeanor and pleasant expression, she projected the truth of Christian hope. Bound to the confines of the internment camp, she knew she was with God and living for him. Two years before her arrest, she composed the following poem:

> Whenever storms are roaring,
> You, Lord, are our support...
> Safe, secure we stand,
> Trusting hold your hand...
> The nations rage in frenzy...
> God is with us here.[53]

Edith wrote these words from behind cloistered walls, but now, in a Nazi concentration camp, she still believed, "God is with us here." One witness reflected that Edith resembled the Sorrowful Mother without her Son.[54] As apt as this description seemed, Edith knew that Mary and Christ are always inseparable. Edith recognized Christ, even in as unlikely a place as an internment camp. "Whatever happens," she said, "I am prepared for it. The dear Child Jesus is among us even here."[55]

Never doubting his presence, Edith continued to embrace the mission he had given her: to let his presence be known. She would seek to "unveil Christ" as she had encouraged women to do so many years before. Edith's actions, her bearing, even her expression, gave testimony to his hidden presence. "Her deep faith," remarked a witness, "created about her an atmosphere of heavenly life."[56] Edith seemed to personify her own words from her Marian poem:

...those whom you have chosen for companions
To stand with you around the eternal throne,
They here must stand with you beneath the cross,
And with the lifeblood of their own bitter pains
Must purchase heavenly glory to those souls
Whom God's Son entrusted to their care.[57]

Like Mary at Cana, Edith surveyed the conditions of her fellow prisoners with a vigilant eye. With a sense of tranquillity, prayerfulness, and compassion, Edith consoled the suffering, including mothers so agonized by their plight they could barely care for their children. Edith came to the children's assistance, washing and feeding them, and combing their hair.[58] Having once given a radio talk in Austria on the "Maternal Art of Rearing Children," she now was exerting a maternal presence to these children, even as the Nazis were preparing to murder them. Edith once expressed concern for orphans, including those whose parents were living but not truly present. She reflected how they needed a loving hand to help them out of their darkness and squalor.

With the same type of maternal love she once used to describe St. Elizabeth of Hungary, Edith reached out in kindness to all the prisoners. Her words regarding St. Elizabeth are almost autobiographical and prophetic:

> From earliest youth she opened her heart in warm, compassionate love for all who suffered and were oppressed. She was moved to feed the hungry and to tend the sick, but was never satisfied with warding off material need alone, always desiring to have cold hearts warm themselves at her own. The poor children in her hospital ran into her arms calling her mother, because they felt her real maternal love.[59]

The children in the camp snuggled in Edith's arms, where they were comforted by her maternal love.

Sister Teresa Benedicta of the Cross did not shun suffering. She was living her vocation of martyrdom and the words she had once written to a friend: "One cannot wish for a deliverance from the cross when one bears the noble title 'of the Cross.'"[60] In her treatise on John of the Cross, Edith had explained that those who wish to

> ...win eternal life, they too must give up their earthly life. They must die with Christ in order to rise with him: the lifelong death of suffering and of daily self-denial, and even, if necessary, the bloody death of a martyr for the gospel of Christ.[61]

As Edith headed to her own death, she walked calmly as a woman of faith who sought to unite her will to the Lord's and her heart to his. Embracing her vocation, she projected a serene demeanor and a mysterious joy. The love of the true spouse of Christ, she once wrote, is "apparent in the instinctive, radiating joyfulness bestowed on a life spent with and for Christ, and the obvious readiness to make sacrifices, and in the inner peace which no external vicissitude can disrupt."[62] Nothing could shake her inner peace, even as she entered the depths of anguish. Like her namesake St. Teresa of Avila, she lived the mystery of joy amidst suffering, as she so eloquently described:

> [B]eing one with Christ is our sanctity, and progressively *becoming* one with him our happiness on earth, the love of the cross in no way contradicts being a joyful child of God. Helping Christ carry his cross fills one with a strong and pure joy, and those who may and can do so, the builders of God's kingdom, are the most authentic children of God.... To suffer and to be happy although suffering, to have one's feet on the earth, to walk on the dirty and rough paths of this earth and yet to be enthroned with Christ at the Father's right hand, to laugh and cry with the children of this world and ceaselessly sing the praises of God with the choirs of angels— this is the life of the Christian until the morning of eternity breaks forth.[63]

Two years earlier, she had spoken about the need to help "the entire parched world;" now in that world, she strove to give living water, introducing others to the face of Christ.[64] She knew that: "Streams of living water flow from all those who live in God's hand." Her belief that those who collaborate with God's work exert a "mysterious magnetic appeal on thirsty souls," led her to exert that influence even in the camps.[65] But she, too, was thirsty: she longed for the Eucharist. Yet her years of Eucharistic living would strengthen her. She wrote powerfully of the longing of John of the Cross to celebrate Mass and receive the Eucharist. In so doing, she revealed her own passionate love for the Eucharistic Lord. "How he must have missed celebrating the holy sacrifice in the nine long months when he was never allowed to do so! He had to spend the Feast of Corpus Christi, on which he was accustomed to kneel for hours in adoration before the Blessed Sacrament, without Mass and Communion."[66] Now, Edith, too, was a prisoner longing for the Eucharist.

Edith heard the call of the Lord amidst chaos and uncertainty; she did not panic but continued to listen for his voice and to see opportunities for doing his will.

In 1938 she had consoled a religious sister who was living in a home without the Blessed Sacrament.

> Certainly it is difficult.... But God is within us after all, the entire Blessed Trinity, if we can but understand how to build within ourselves a well-locked cell and withdraw there as often as possible, then we will lack nothing anywhere in the world. That, after all, is how the priests and religious in prison must help themselves. For those who grasp this it becomes a time of great grace.[67]

For Edith, this indeed was a time of great grace. Despite her suffering, she knew that God was calling her to deeper intimacy. She wrote from the Westerbork internment camp, five days before she died in Auschwitz: "We are very calm and cheerful. Of course, so far there has been no Mass and Communion; maybe that will come later. Now we have a chance to experience a little how to live purely from within."[68] She was "able to pray gloriously."[69]

She once explained: "...when the Lord comes to me then in Holy Communion, then I may ask him, 'Lord, what do you want of me?' (St. Teresa)."[70]

Although she could not receive Communion in the camps, she focused on St. Teresa's question: "Lord, what do you want of me?" With a sense of resolve and composure, she realized that the answer was to remain a prisoner; she could not escape. She knew, as she often pondered, that true growth in Christian maturity would entail some measure of the agony of Gethsemane, the *Via Dolorosa*, and Golgotha.[71] In many ways, Edith Stein's Gethsemane came long before the internment camp— she walked the way of the cross throughout her Christian life, and gave her fiat with each step that led her closer to the cross and to her death in Auschwitz.

Years before, Edith had spoken about the fear of "falling prey to nothingness."[72] She conquered that fear by a trust in the "sheltering hold" of the arms of God.[73] Heading to Auschwitz on August 7, 1942, she trusted that God's strong arms were carrying her—as she sought to carry his life. She would fall prey to the Nazis, but not to nothingness.

Her story is one of darkness and light, silence and speech, sorrow and joy, the cross and the resurrection. Hers is a story of consistency—the consistent calling of God. Even in the camps, God was calling Edith, just as he had called her in the classroom, the lecture halls, and the convent. He now had sent her back to a world of suffering and evil that needed healing and redemption. She would do her part alongside Christ, who had summoned her to his cross. He was calling her to make him present to others, to carry his life into the world. Edith had not failed in this vocation during her life, and she would not fail on her way to death. Her journey to Auschwitz was filled with meaning. She had surrendered her life to Christ, and she went to her death confident that God had accepted her sacrifice. She lived out her message to her fellow Sisters, "Surrender without reservation to the Lord who has called us. This is required of us so that the face of the earth may be renewed."[74]

Twelve years earlier she recognized the "urgency" of her own "*holocaustum*," and she continued to participate in the power of redemptive suffering all the way to a Nazi gas chamber.[75] In her Carmelite habit, Sister Teresa Benedicta of the Cross entered the gates of Auschwitz. Along with the other prisoners, the guards immediately forced Edith to undress completely. Then they shoved all of them into a "shower."

Alongside Rosa, Edith walked into a nondescript building that would become a terror-filled chamber of death. After the doors clanged shut, noxious fumes permeated the room. The poisonous gas robbed the sisters and their fellow prisoners of their remaining breaths. Their deaths, however, would not signal the triumph of hatred.

Edith's life had been extinguished, but the fruits of her love survived. She once had urged a religious sister to give her whole life to Christ so that at the end of her life she could echo the words of St. Thérèse of Lisieux: "I do not regret that I have given myself to love."[76] Surely Edith herself had no such regrets, having confidently and passionately given herself to divine love. She was convinced that with God's grace, her self-sacrificial love would bear fruit for the kingdom of God, even if she never saw the fruits of her work. She had explained:

> In faithful trust, we must abandon our souls to the sovereignty of the Holy Spirit. It is not necessary that we experience the epiphany in our lives. We may live in confident certainty that the Spirit of God secretly effects

its fruits in the kingdom of God. We will see them in eternity.

With quiet resolve, Sister Teresa Benedicta of the Cross gave herself to Love, preparing for her death with confidence in the secret workings of God—the mystery of his love in the mystery of the cross.

Epilogue: Edith Stein's Message for Today

At the dawn of the new millennium, I exited a bus and began a memorable walk through the woods. I was traveling with approximately twenty-five fellow pilgrims under the guidance of Father John Sullivan, O.C.D. We were asked to proceed in silence, collect our thoughts, pray, and remember.

We were all very conscious of the sound of our footsteps breaking the disconcerting silence, and we were aware of the peculiar beauty of our surroundings and the spectacular majesty of the tall birch trees for which the place was named: Birkenau—that is, Auschwitz-Birkenau. I had not expected to find any beauty in this place haunted by the evil that had occurred there. The juxtaposition unsettled me.

I tried to imagine Edith traveling on the train to this death camp. Not all prisoners survived the grueling journey from Westerbork camp. Herded into the train like animals, the prisoners must have felt buried alive.

They had no food or water and no room to move. They had to gasp for air. Did they panic? Faint? Weep? Pray? Did Edith lead them in prayer? Were they comforted by this Carmelite nun? Were they consoled by her presence? I was awestruck that Edith could maintain her prayerful composure every step along the way to her death. When she had learned that she would be sent to a labor camp, she had steadied herself, resolving to "work and pray,"[1] to keep her eyes focused on Christ. She would be strong, just as she had been while a nurse during World War I. At that time, she had not feared any type of contamination—neither from disease (though lice made her hesitate!) nor from the immorality around her. Now Edith again was unafraid of being poisoned by the evils around her. Resolved to remain uncontaminated, she would exert a positive influence in the camps, having prepared herself to bring God's love wherever she was sent.

The train heading to Auschwitz stopped in Schifferstadt, the town where her first spiritual director, Father Joseph Schwind, had lived. Through a small opening between the wooden slats of the train car, Edith tossed a message to his family saying that she was heading to Poland.[2] One of her last messages, then, was directed to the relatives of the priest who guided her spiritual journey as she came to love Christ, the Way, the Truth, and the Life.

The sign at the entrance to Auschwitz, "Work shall set you free," stood in stark contrast to the life of a woman of faith who embraced the Gospel passage, "Truth shall set you free." As I stood in the place of deceit and death,

I pondered Edith's ever-deepening relationship to Truth.

I knelt in prayer with my fellow travelers at the site of a gas chamber where Edith and her sister Rosa were gassed to death on August 9, 1942. Walking away from the site, I thought of the final days of Edith's life as well as her early childhood. I recalled an incident in Edith's youth when she and her sister Erna nearly died. They had accidentally left a gas lamp burning as they drifted off to sleep. The gas was slowly poisoning them. The following morning their sister Elfriede opened their bedroom door and was horrified to find them in a semi-conscious stupor and "deathly white...."[3] Quickly opening the windows and shaking her sisters into consciousness, Elfriede saved them from certain death. Approximately three decades later, there was no one to save Edith and her sister Rosa from the poisonous fumes of the gas chamber.

On the way to Auschwitz, Rosa and Edith traveled with two of Edith's close friends—her godchildren Ruth Kantorowicz and Alice Reis, people she had introduced to an ever-deepening relationship with Christ. Edith had much experience in walking with others through life's vicissitudes, and vast experience in suffering with others. She knew how to create community, even in difficult situations. She would act no differently in the camps; she would live her final days on earth in communion with others.

Always concerned about Ruth Kantorowicz's frail nature, Edith once had noted that Ruth was "fearfully helpless." She had assisted Ruth in her effort to enter the convent, and even more when the religious community did not accept her. Expressing her sympathy for Ruth, Edith had commented that "someone would have to take her by the hand now and help her to get a foothold in the world again." She had noted that Ruth needed to stand "on her own two feet," because "in the present situation...the suspicion arises that she is only seeking a refuge [in the convent]. But one cannot expect a little rabbit to behave like a lion."[4] I wondered if Edith held Ruth's hand as they boarded the train to Auschwitz; perhaps she held her hand as they entered the gas chamber, not like rabbits or lions, but like lambs led to the slaughter.

We sat silently on the bus as we left Auschwitz for Edith Stein's home in Wroclaw, Poland (formerly Breslau, Germany). When I stepped into the parlor where Edith had spent so much time writing, I found myself brushing away tears. I had seen where she died; and now I stood in the room where she had dreamed of doing something great with her life.

The life and death of Edith Stein continue to have meaning for us, a meaning that transcends time and place. Her spiritual legacy certainly has meant a great deal to me, for she has helped me to understand my faith better and to appreciate more deeply God's blessings, and for this, I am in her debt.

Since my return from the pilgrimage to Germany, I have often pondered Edith Stein's message for today's society. This was particularly true after the events of September 11, 2001. Only a few weeks after the tragic attack, I walked the city streets that were once so familiar but now seemed like a foreign land. I was reminded of the reality of evil in the world.

Together with countless others, I stood before the makeshift altars, the posters of missing loved ones, and the candles burning in memory of those who had perished. The faces around me reflected the horror we all felt. We stood aghast at the site of the terrorist attack, mourning lives lost, lives harmed, and lives changed forever. We stared at the posters of missing loved ones and wept for people we had never met. I remember the eerie silence. Countless men and women converged, and yet one could actually feel the silence. I noticed people making the Sign of the Cross and their lips moving as they offered a quiet prayer. A musician strummed his guitar very gently and reverently, as if he were playing in a church rather than on a city street.

The air was still heavy with smoke, and my eyes began to sting from the wind-blown ashes and my tears. I looked up and suddenly saw an image on a building: Mary holding the Infant Jesus. I was standing next to the church of Our Lady of Victories.

Aware of the chaos and horror only steps away, I felt a strange sense of security and hope under the gaze of Mary and her Son. I entered the vestibule of the church and saw a bronze sculpture of St. Edith Stein standing at the foot of the cross, her eyes fixed on the crucified body of Christ and her comforting arms embracing little children.

Here was a testament to Edith's profound understanding of Mary's mission to stand by the Redeemer and, "with the lifeblood of her own bitter pains," to obtain heavenly glory for those souls God entrusted to her care. Edith believed that she should imitate Mary, and she was confident that her own suffering would be life affirming and life giving.

Edith followed the spiritual motherhood of the Mother of God, who cared for the body of Christ from the moment of his conception to his death on the cross, and who continues to care for his Mystical Body. St. Teresa Benedicta of the Cross strove to be wedded to the cross while caring for the souls entrusted to her, even in Auschwitz. Her words echo to us in the twenty-first century: "Today, I stood with you beneath the cross." Her words pose the questions: Today, have we stood beneath the cross? Today, have *I* stood beneath the cross?

Edith's life, extinguished in a gas chamber, points us to the Spirit, who breathes eternal life. Edith knew this well:

> Wherever [the Spirit] was once at work in forming human lives and human structures, it leaves behind... a mysterious existence, like hidden and carefully tended embers that flare up brightly, glow and ignite as soon as a living breath blows on them. The lovingly penetrating gaze of the researcher who traces out the hidden sparks from the monuments of the past—this is the living breath that lets the flame flare up. Receptive human souls are the stuff in which it ignites and becomes the informing strength that helps in mastering and shaping present life.... From the original source of all fire and light, the hidden embers are mysteriously nourished and preserved in order to break out again and again as an inexhaustible, productive source of blessing.[5]

God blessed Edith with the ability to respond with strength and love in the darkest of times. She asked for the grace to love, and God not only helped her to act lovingly, but he also gave her his own boundless love.

Edith Stein reminds us that with God's help we can be strong, faithful Christians capable of standing at the foot of the cross with Mary. Even with broken hearts, we can be pillars of strength to suffering humanity. We can make a positive impact on the Church and on society. In addition, St. Edith Stein reminds us that we can fulfill our unique vocations when we adopt and live out the words of the Blessed Virgin Mary at the dawning of the first millennium: "Let it be done unto me according to your word."

Let us pray that God's life may "Easter" in us, so that we, like Edith Stein, may carry his life into the world:[6]

For those of us who have experienced dissension
 and strife,
let Christ, the Prince of Peace, Easter in us!
May he give us quietness of heart.

For those of us who have suffered deceits and lies,
let Christ, the Truth, Easter in us!
May he teach us the truth of his love.

For those of us who have a difficult time forgiving—
 forgiving others or ourselves,
let Christ, the Merciful Lord, Easter in us!
May he draw us ever nearer to his compassionate
 heart.

For those of us who struggle with self-esteem—
 a feeling of lack of worth—
let his Majesty, the King of Glory, Easter in us!
May he remind us of our royal dignity.

For those of us who have experienced betrayals,
let Jesus, the Divine Friend, Easter in us!
May he introduce us to his intimate friendship,
and to people whose holy friendships will bring us
closer to God and neighbor.

For those of us who struggle to find the right words
to say,
let Jesus, the Word himself, Easter in us!
May he give us the gift of speech—speech that is
holy, good, and affirming of God-given life.

For those of us who suffer illness—of mind, heart,
body—
let God, the Divine Physician, Easter in us!
May he touch us with his gift of healing.

For those of us who experience the stress of
scholarly endeavors,
let Jesus, the Teacher, Easter in us!
May he give us the gift of recollected study time,
and the gift to express our thoughts readily
and clearly.

For those of us who have lost direction or are searching
for the right path,
Let Jesus, the Way, the Truth, and the Life, Easter in us!
May he help us to see where he is directing us,
and may we follow him with steadfast devotion.

For those of us who have experienced hatred
or violence to body, heart, or mind,
Let God, Love himself, Easter in us!

May he introduce us to his great love, and may his love shine forth in our daily lives!

God is alive!
May he Easter in us!
Today, let us carry his life into the world!

St. Edith Stein, pray for us.
Amen.

Acknowledgments

For more than a decade, I have been encouraged and supported by friends and family as I have delved into the life and spirituality of Edith Stein. I am grateful to those who have walked with me, collaborating in their own unique ways, particularly Rev. Monsignor Kevin Royal; Carol Pinard; Kathleen Venters; Janice Pedicino; Gregory Tobin; Dr. Susan Timoney; and my primary cheerleaders, Janice and Jeanne Traflet; and, most especially, my Mom. They all listened good-naturedly, never seeming to tire of the Edith Stein story, as they urged me to continue my research, writing, and public speaking. I also have been inspired by the friendship and the work of Rev. John Sullivan, O.C.D., and have been edified by his love of Carmelite spirituality and his vast knowledge of St. Edith Stein. My understanding and love of Edith Stein was further influenced by the translations and commentaries of Sr. Josephine Koeppel, O.C.D.; I am awed by Sister's expertise, inspired by her religious life, and touched by her kind encouragement of this project.

During my research, I have been blessed with supportive colleagues at Immaculate Conception Seminary School of Theology who often asked for progress reports, encouraged my research, and offered prayers, particularly Rev. Monsignor Robert Coleman, Rev. Monsignor Thomas Nydegger, Rev. Joseph Chapel, Very Rev. John Russell, O.Carm., Rev. Monsignor Gerard McCarren, Dr. Gregory Glazov, Ewa Bracko, and Diane Carr. I am thankful to other members of the seminary community, and alumni, too, who read each chapter of this book, giving wonderful suggestions and helpful edits, including Kristine Hudak, Kimberly Benson, Stella Wilkins, Julie Burkey, Elizabeth Brevetti, and Stephen and Sarah Nakrosis.

To all the seminarians from 1999 to 2008 who have listened to so many of my talks on Edith Stein—thank you! I'm particularly grateful to Rev. Esterminio Chica, who even after graduation and ordination continued to ask for a book on Edith and urged me to write it. To seminarians Brian Quinn and Robert McLaughlin, thank you for reviewing every sentence meticulously and even cheerfully. Edith Stein encouraged many seminarians on their paths to the priesthood; she listened to their practice homilies; prayed for them; and, on at least one occasion, offered advice on a thesis. Approximately seventy-five years later, you carefully considered Edith's writing (and mine!); may Edith's spiritual journey inspire yours.

I am indebted to the staff of Pauline Books & Media who have worked with me during these recent years, including Kate Hux, Tiffany Fox, Sarah Erlandson, Brad McCracken, Debra Lavelle, and Lindsey Macauley.

Mostly, I appreciate the patience, counsel, and professional expertise of Sr. Marianne Lorraine, FSP; Sr. Madonna Ratliff, FSP; and Sr. Maria Grace, FSP. They not only assisted me throughout the process of writing; they introduced me to the spirituality of the Daughters of St. Paul. While their kind advice has shaped the content of this book about Edith's journey, their spiritual lives have inspired my own life's journey, and I am very grateful.

I would also like to thank the Institute of Carmelite Studies for the use of material from the following publications:

From *On the Problem of Empathy* by Edith Stein. Translated by Waltraut Stein, Ph.D. Copyright © 1989 by Washington Province of Discalced Carmelites ICS Publications 2131 Lincoln Road NE, Washington, DC 20002-1199 U.S.A. www.icspublications.org

From *Essays on Woman* by Edith Stein. Translated by Freda Mary Oben, Ph.D. Copyright © 1987, 1996 Washington Province of Discalced Carmelites ICS Publications 2131 Lincoln Road NE, Washington, DC 20002-1199 U.S.A. www.icspublications.org

From *Self-Portrait in Letters* by Edith Stein. Translated by Josephine Koeppel, O.C.D. Copyright © 1993 Washington Province of Discalced Carmelites ICS Publications 2131 Lincoln Road NE, Washington, DC 20002-1199 U.S.A. www.icspublications.org

From *Life in a Jewish Family* by Edith Stein. Translated by Josephine Koeppel, O.C.D. Copyright © 1986 by Washington Province of Discalced Carmelites ICS Publications 2131 Lincoln Road NE, Washington, DC 20002-1199 U.S.A. www.icspublications.org

From *The Hidden Life* by Edith Stein. Translated by Waltraut Stein, Ph.D. Copyright © 1992 by Washington Province of Discalced Carmelites ICS Publication 2131 Lincoln Road NE, Washington, DC 20002-1199 U.S.A. www.icspublications.org

From *Finite and Eternal Being* by Edith Stein. Translated by Kurt F. Reinhardt © 2002 by Washington Province of Discalced Carmelites ICS Publications 2131 Lincoln Road NE, Washington, DC 20002-1151 U.S.A. www.icspublications.org

From *The Science of the Cross* by Edith Stein. Translated by Josephine Koeppel, O.C.D. © 2003 by Washington Province of Discalced Carmelites ICS Publications 2131 Lincoln Road NE, Washington, DC 20002-1151 U.S.A. www.ics-publications.org

From *Never Forget,* edited by Waltraude Herbstrith, OCD. Translated by Susanne Batzdorff © 1998 by Washington Province of Discalced Carmelites ICS Publications 2131 Lincoln Road NE, Washington, DC 20002-1151 U.S.A. www.icspublications.org

From *Edith Stein: The Life of a Philosopher and Carmelite* by Teresia Renata Posselt, O.C.D. Edited by Susanne Batzdorff, Josephine Koeppel and John Sullivan © 2005 by Washington Province of Discalced Carmelites ICS Publications 2131 Lincoln Road NE, Washington, DC20002-1155 U.S.A. www.icspublications.org

Notes

Introduction:
The Challenge of Beginnings

1. Edith Stein, *Finite and Eternal Being: An Attempt at an Ascent to the Meaning of Being*, translation of *Endliches und Ewiges Sein*, translated by Kurt Reinhardt, *Collected Works of Edith Stein* Vol. 9, (Washington, DC: ICS Publications, 2002), author's preface, xxvii. (Hereafter cited as *Finite and Eternal Being.*)

2. Letter no. 89, to Sr. Adelgundis Jaegerschmid, O.S.B., April 28, 1931, in *Self-Portrait in Letters, 1916–1942*, by Edith Stein, translated by Josephine Koeppel, edited by L. Gelber and Romaeous Leuven (Washington, DC: ICS Publications, 1993). (Hereafter cited as *Self-Portrait.*)

CHAPTER 1
Carrying Divine Life into the World

1. Edith Stein, *Life in a Jewish Family, 1891–1916*, translated by Josephine Koeppel, edited by L. Gelber and Romaeous Leuven (Washington, DC: ICS Publications, 1986), 72 (hereafter cited as *Life*).

2. *Life*, 74.
3. Ibid.
4. Ibid., 138.
5. Ibid., 139.
6. Ibid.
7. Ibid.
8. Ibid., 145.
9. Ibid., 148.
10. Ibid., 90.
11. Ibid., 150.
12. Ibid.
13. Ibid., 316.
14. Ibid., 60.
15. Ibid., 152.
16. Ibid., 155.
17. Ibid., 218.
18. Ibid.
19. Ibid.
20. Ibid.
21. Ibid., 220.
22. Ibid., 195.
23. Ibid.
24. Ibid.
25. Ibid., 195–96.
26. Ibid., 259.
27. Ibid., 254.
28. Ibid., 284.
29. Ibid., 297.
30. Ibid.
31. Ibid.
32. Ibid., 319.

33. Ibid., 348.

34. Ibid., 340.

35. Ibid., 338.

36. Ibid.

37. Ibid.

38. Letter no. 181, to Ruth Kantorowicz, October 4, 1934, in *Self-Portrait.*

39. Letter no. 123, to Sr. Callista Kopf, October 20, 1932, in *Self-Portrait.*

40. Letter no. 52, to Sr. Adelgundis Jaegerschmid, February 16, 1930, in *Self-Portrait.*

41. Letter no. 45, to Sr. Callista Kopf, February 12, 1928, in *Self-Portrait.*

42. *Finite and Eternal Being,* 58–59.

43. Letter no. 45, to Sr. Callista Kopf, February 12, 1928, in *Self-Portrait.*

44. Letter no. 73, to Ottilie Küchenhoff, December 7, 1930, in *Self-Portrait.*

45. Letter no. 89, to Sr. Adelgundis Jaegerschmid, April 28, 1931, in *Self-Portrait.*

46. Teresia Renata Posselt, O.C.D., *Edith Stein: The Life of a Philosopher and Carmelite,* edited by Susanne Batzdorff, Josephine Koeppel, and John Sullivan (Washington, DC: ICS Publications, 2005), 197 (hereafter cited as *Edith Stein*).

47. "The Hidden Life and Epiphany," in *The Hidden Life,* edited by L. Gelber and Michael Linssen, translated by Waltraut Stein (Washington, DC: ICS Publications, 1992), 110 (hereafter cited as *Hidden Life*).

48. "The Hidden Life and Epiphany," in *Hidden Life,* 111.

49. Ibid.

50. "Love for Love: The Life and Works of St. Teresa of Jesus," in *Hidden Life,* 29.

51. Ibid.

52. Letter no. 45, to Sr. Callista Kopf, February 12, 1928, in *Self-Portrait.*

53. Letter no. 93a, to Fritz Kaufmann, June 14, 1931, in *Self-Portrait.*

54. Letter no. 156, to Gertrud von le Fort, October 9, 1933, in *Self-Portrait.*

55. "And I Remain with You: From a Pentecost Novena," in *Hidden Life,* 141.

56. "The Hidden Life and Epiphany," in *Hidden Life,* 109.

57. "Elevation of the Cross: September 14, 1939: *Ave Crux, Spes Unica!*" in *Hidden Life,* 95–96.

58. Ibid., 96.

59. Ibid.

60. *Edith Stein,* 218.

61. Ibid., 214, citing testimony of Pierre Cuypers and Piet O. van Kempen.

CHAPTER 2

Searching for the Truth:
Edith Stein's Spiritual Quest

1. *Life,* 148.

2. Ibid., 150.

3. Ibid., 155.

4. Ibid., 155–56.

5. Ibid., 173.

6. Ibid.

7. Ibid., 172.

8. Ibid., 183.

9. Ibid., 216–17.

10. Ibid., 260–61.

11. *Finite and Eternal Being,* 60.

12. *Life,* 213.

13. Ibid., 399.

14. Ibid., 277.

15. Max Scheler's philosophical works were the subject of the 1954 doctoral dissertation of Karol Wojtyla, later Pope John Paul II. The dissertation was titled, "An Evaluation of the Possibility of Constructing a Christian Ethics on the Basis of the System of Max Scheler."

16. *Life,* 259.

17. Ibid., 260.

18. Ibid.

19. Ibid., 261.

20. "I Am Always in Your Midst" in *Hidden Life,* 119.

21. *Life,* 294.

22. Ibid., 385.

23. Ibid., 377–85.

24. Ibid., 401.

25. Ibid.

26. Ibid.

27. Ibid., 401–402.

28. Letter no. 4, to Fritz Kaufmann, January 12, 1917, in *Self-Portrait.*

29. *Life,* 284.

30. *Edith Stein,* 59–60.

31. Edith Stein, *On the Problem of Empathy,* translated by Waltraut Stein, Ph.D. (Washington, DC: ICS Publications, 1989), 117.

32. The exact date of this reading is not known, just that it was years before she read the *Autobiography of Teresa of Avila.*

33. *Life,* 235.

34. Ibid., 238.

35. Ibid., 237.

36. Ibid.

37. Gerhard Stein, "My Experiences with My Aunt Edith," in *Never Forget*, edited by Waltraude Herbstrith, O.C.D., translated by Susanne Batzdorff, (Washington DC: ICS Publications, 1998), 53–4.

38. Fr. Ulrich Dobhan, cited in "Edith Stein's Conversion Was No Coincidence," http://zenit.org/article-18865?l=english.

39. "A Chosen Vessel of Divine Wisdom: Sr. Marie-Aimee de Jesus," in *Hidden Life*, 79.

40. Letter no. 105, to Erna Hermann, September 8, 1931, in *Self-Portrait*.

41. "The Hidden Life and Epiphany," in *Hidden Life*, 10–11.

42. "*Te Deum Laudamus*: For December 7, 1940 (St. Ambrose)," in *Hidden Life*, 124.

43. Letter no. 158, to Gertrud von le Fort, October 17, 1933, in *Self-Portrait*.

44. See *Edith Stein*, 118; 124-129.

45. Ibid., 78.

46. Letter no. 104, to Rose Magold, August 30, 1931, in *Self-Portrait*.

47. *Edith Stein*, 118.

48. Letter no. 102, to Anneliese Lichtenberger, August 17, 1931, in *Self-Portrait*.

49. Letter no. 181, to Ruth Kantorowicz, October 4, 1934, in *Self-Portrait*.

50. Letter no. 102, to Anneliese Lichtenberger, August 17, 1931, in *Self-Portrait*.

51. Letter no. 181, to Ruth Kantorowicz, October 4, 1934, in *Self-Portrait*.

52. Letter no. 42a, to Fritz Kaufmann, January 6, 1927, in *Self-Portrait*.

53. Letter no. 38a, to Fritz Kaufmann, September 13, 1925, in *Self-Portrait*.

54. Letter no. 45, to Sr. Callista Kopf, February 12, 1928, in *Self-Portrait*.

55. Ibid.

56. *Edith Stein*, 72.

57. Letter no. 89, to Sr. Adelgundis Jaegerschmid, April 28, 1931, in *Self-Portrait*.

58. Ibid.

59. Letter no. 45, to Sr. Callista Kopf, February 12, 1928, in *Self-Portrait*.

60. *Edith Stein*, 67.

61. Letter no. 63, to Erna Hermann, September 16, 1930, in *Self-Portrait*.

62. Letter no. 76, to Erna Hermann, December 19, 1930, in *Self-Portrait*.

63. "I Am Always in Your Midst," in *Hidden Life*, 119–20.

64. Edith Stein, "Spirituality of the Christian Woman," *Essays on Woman*, translated by Freda Mary Oben, Ph.D. (Washington DC: ICS Publications, 1996), 126–27. (Hereafter cited as *Woman*.)

65. Ibid., 126.

66. *Edith Stein*, 78.

67. "The Hidden Life and Epiphany," in *Hidden Life*, 109.

68. Letter no. 93a, to Fritz Kaufmann, June 14, 1931, in *Self-Portrait*.

69. Letter no. 167, to Sr. Adelgundis Jaegerschmid, March 20, 1934, in *Self-Portrait*.

CHAPTER 3

Loving with His Love:
The Importance of the Eucharist

1. *Life*, 24.

2. Letter no. 45, to Sr. Callista Kopf, February 12, 1928, in *Self-Portrait*.

3. "Ethos of Women's Professions," in *Woman*, 56.

4. Ibid.

5. Letter no. 45, to Sr. Callista Kopf, February 12, 1928, in *Self-Portrait.*

6. Ibid.

7. "Ethos of Women's Professions," in *Woman,* 56.

8. Ibid., 56–57.

9. "Principles of Women's Education," in *Woman,* 138–39.

10. *Life,* 401.

11. Letter no. 92, to Anna Bosslet, May 11, 1931, in *Self-Portrait.*

12. "Principles of Women's Education" in *Woman,* 143–44.

13. Ibid., 144.

14. "Spirituality of the Christian Woman," in *Woman,* 125.

15. See letter no. 87, to Sr. Callista Kopf, March 28, 1931, in *Self-Portrait.* See also letter no. 89, to Sr. Adelgundis Jaegerschmid, April 28, 1931, in *Self-Portrait.*

16. *Edith Stein,* 118.

17. Ibid., 111.

18. Ibid., 104.

19. "St. Teresa Margaret of the Sacred Heart," in *Hidden Life,* 68.

20. *Edith Stein,* 70.

21. Ibid., 69.

22. Letter no. 123, to Sr. Callista Kopf, October 20, 1932, in *Self-Portrait.*

23. *Edith Stein,* 72.

24. Ibid., 85.

25. Ibid.

26. Ibid., 113.

27. Ibid., 118.

28. Ibid.

29. Ibid., 152.

30. Ibid., 119.

31. Ibid., 120.

32. Ibid.

33. Ibid., 121.

34. Letter no. 152, to Sr. Adelgundis Jaegerschmid, August 27, 1933, in *Self-Portrait*.

35. *Edith Stein*, 124.

36. Ibid.

37. Ibid.

38. Ibid.

39. Letter no. 156, to Gertrud von le Fort, October 9, 1933, in *Self-Portrait*.

40. Letter no. 160, to Hedwig Conrad-Martius, Edith's godmother, October 31, 1933, in *Self-Portrait*.

41. See "The Road to Carmel," in *Edith Stein*, 126–27. See also Suzanne Batzdorff, "A Martyr of Auschwitz," *The New York Times Magazine*, April 12, 1987: 110.

42. *Edith Stein*, 126.

43. Ibid.

44. Ibid., 128.

45. Letter no. 160, to Hedwig Conrad-Martius, October 31, 1933, in *Self-Portrait*.

46. See *Edith Stein*, 128.

47. Ibid., 129.

48. Ibid., 130.

49. Letter no. 174, to Fritz Kaufmann, May 14, 1934, in *Self-Portrait*.

50. Letter no. 158a, to Fritz Kaufmann, October 17, 1933, in *Self-Portrait*.

51. "Love for Love: Life and Works of St. Teresa of Jesus," in *Hidden Life*, 37.

52. "On the History and Spirit of Carmel," in *Hidden Life*, 6.

53. Letter no. 295, to Sr. Maria Mechtildis Welter, February 21, 1939, in *Self-Portrait*.

54. Letter no. 183, to Gisela Naegeli, Autumn 1934, in *Self-Portrait*.

55. Letter no. 164, to Sr. Adelgundis Jaegerschmid, January 11, 1934, in *Self-Portrait.*

56. Ibid.

57. Letter no. 192, to Gertrud von le Fort, January 31, 1935, in *Self-Portrait.*

58. "Life for Love: The Life and Works of St. Teresa of Jesus," in *Hidden Life,* 29.

59. Letter no. 183, to Gisela Naegeli, Autumn 1934, in *Self-Portrait.*

60. *Edith Stein,* 180–81.

61. "I Will Remain with You..." in *Hidden Life,* 137.

62. "Ethos of Women's Professions," in *Woman,* 56.

63. "I Will Remain with You..." in *Hidden Life,* 137, 139.

64. "The Prayer of the Church," in *Hidden Life,* 10.

65. Ibid., 10–11.

66. "I Will Remain with You..." in *Hidden Life,* 139.

67. "Exaltation of the Cross, September 14, 1941," in *Hidden Life,* 102–103.

68. *Edith Stein,* 184.

69. Letter no. 300, to Mother Petra Brüning, April 16, 1939, in *Self-Portrait.*

70. "For January 6, 1941," in *Hidden Life,* 115.

71. Ibid.

72. Ibid.

CHAPTER 4

Carrying Divine Life:
The Example of Mary

1. "Vocations of Man and Woman," in *Woman,* 70.

2. "Problems of Women's Education," in *Woman,* 201.

3. "The Prayer of the Church," in *Hidden Life,* 15.

4. See "Church, Woman, and Youth," in *Woman*, 240–41.

5. Ibid., 241.

6. "Problems of Women's Education," in *Woman*, 198–99. See also *Finite and Eternal Being*, 516–17.

7. "Problems of Women's Education," in *Woman*, 200

8. Ibid. See also *Finite and Eternal Being*, 516–17.

9. Outline for "Ethos of Women's Profession," in Editor's Introduction, *Woman*, 23.

10. "The Prayer of the Church," in *Hidden Life*, 13.

11. See Editor's Introduction, in *Woman*, 23.

12. "The Prayer of the Church," in *Hidden Life*, 12.

13. Ibid., 13.

14. "For the First Profession of Sr. Miriam of Little St. Thérèse," in *Hidden Life*, 106.

15. Ibid.

16. "Problems of Women's Education," in *Woman*, 200. See also *Finite and Eternal Being*, 516–517.

17. "For the First Profession of Sr. Miriam of Little St. Thérèse" in *Hidden Life*, 106.

18. See *Woman*, 107.

19. Ibid.

20. "The Significance of Woman's Intrinsic Value in National Life," in *Woman*, 265.

21. "The Prayer of the Church," in *Hidden Life*, 13.

22. Ibid.

23. "Problems of Women's Education," in *Woman*, 198.

24. "Ethos of Women's Professions," in *Woman*, 47.

25. "Problems of Women's Education," in *Woman*, 198. See also "Ethos of Women's Professions," in *Woman*, 47.

26. "Problems of Women's Education," in *Woman*, 198.

27. Editor's Introduction, in *Woman*, 24.

28. "Woman as Guide in the Church," in *Woman*, 36.

29. "The Significance of Woman's Intrinsic Value in National Life," in *Woman*, 41.

30. Editor's Introduction, in *Woman*, 24.

31. "Woman as Guide in the Church," in *Woman*, 36.

32. Outline of "Ethos of Women's Professions," in Editor's Introduction, in *Woman*, 24.

33. "The Significance of Woman's Intrinsic Value in National Life," in *Woman*, 264.

34. "Ethos of Women's Professions," in *Woman*, 51.

35. Ibid., 50–51; and "The Significance of Woman's Intrinsic Value in National Life," in *Woman*, 263–265.

36. "The Significance of Women's Intrinsic Value in National Life," in *Woman*, 39.

37. Editor's Introduction, in *Woman*, 23.

38. "Woman as Guide in the Church," in *Woman*, 36.

39. "Love of the Cross: Some Thoughts for the Feast of St. John of the Cross," in *Hidden Life*, 92.

40. "Problems of Women's Education" in *Woman*, 199.

41. Ibid., 198.

42. "The Hidden Life and Epiphany," in *Hidden Life*, 110.

43. Ibid.

44. Editor's Introduction, in *Woman*, 23.

45. *Edith Stein*, 82.

46. See "The Road to Carmel," in *Edith Stein*, 121.

47. Letter no. 222, to Mother Petra Brüning, July 19, 1936, in *Self-Portrait*. Letter no. 223, to Sr. Agnella Stadtmüller, August 9, 1936, in *Self-Portrait*.

48. Letter no. 231, to Hedwig Conrad-Martius, January 13, 1937, in *Self-Portrait*.

49. *Edith Stein*, 171.

50. Letter no. 246, to Sr. Callista Kopf, October 15, 1937, in *Self-Portrait*. See also letter no. 245, to Mother Petra Brüning, September 24, 1937, in *Self-Portrait*.

51. Letter no. 246, to Sr. Callista Kopf, October 15, 1937, in *Self-Portrait*.

52. *"Juxta Crucem Tecum Stare!,"* in *Edith Stein*, 84, citing translated text by Sr. M. Julian, R.S.M., "Edith Stein and the Mother of God," in *Cross and Crown* 8 (1956) 423–444.

53. Letter no. 281, to Mother Petra Brüning, October 31, 1938, in *Self-Portrait*.

54. Ibid.

55. "The Hidden Life and Epiphany," in *Hidden Life*, 112.

56. Letter no. 311, to Sr. Agnella Stadtmüller, March 30, 1940, in *Self-Portrait*.

57. "Exaltation of the Cross, September 14, 1941," in *Hidden Life*, 104.

58. "Conversation at Night," in *Hidden Life*, 129.

59. Ibid., 130–131.

60. Letter no. 164, to Sr. Adelgundis Jaegerschmid, January 11, 1934, in *Self-Portrait*.

61. Letter no. 327, to Mother Johanna van Weersth, November 11, 1941, in *Self-Portrait*.

62. *The Science of the Cross*, translated by Josephine Koeppel, O.C.D. (Washington DC: ICS Publications, 2003), 15, (hereafter cited as *Science of the Cross*).

63. "For the First Profession of Sr. Miriam of Little St. Thérèse," in *Hidden Life*, 108.

CHAPTER 5

Carrying the Cross into a World in Flames

1. "On the History and Spirit of Carmel," in *Hidden Life*, 6. See also *Finite and Eternal Being*, 59–60.

2. "For the First Profession of Sr. Miriam of Little St. Thérèse," in *Hidden Life*, 107.

3. "Elevation of the Cross, September 14, 1939: *Ave Crux, Spes Unica!*," in *Hidden Life*, 95.

4. *Science of the Cross*, 276.

5. Ibid., 18.

6. Ibid., 17.

7. "The Prayer of the Church," in *Hidden Life*, 12.

8. Ibid., 11.

9. *Science of the Cross*, 33.

10. "On the History and Spirit of Carmel," in *Hidden Life*, 6.

11. "*Te Deum Laudamus*: For December 7, 1940 (St. Ambrose)," in *Hidden Life*, 124.

12. *Science of the Cross*, 65.

13. "The Prayer of the Church," in *Hidden Life*, 17.

14. *Edith Stein*, 195.

15. "Love of the Cross: Some Thoughts for the Feast of St. John of the Cross," in *Hidden Life*, 92.

16. Ibid.

17. Letter no. 129, to Anneliese Lichtenberger, December 26, 1932, in *Self-Portrait*.

18. "The Road to Carmel," in *Edith Stein*, 115.

19. Ibid.

20. Ibid., 116.

21. Ibid.

22. *Edith Stein*, 313.

23. In 1937, Pope Pius XI issued *Mit Brennender Sorge*, an encyclical letter condemning racial theories and policies, though Nazism was not specified by name.

24. "The Road to Carmel," in *Edith Stein*, 127.

25. Letter no. 129, to Anneliese Lichtenberger, December 26, 1932, in *Self-Portrait*.

26. Letter no. 287, to Mother Petra Brüning, December 9, 1938, in *Self-Portrait*.

27. Letter no. 148, to Anneliese Lichtenberger, July 26, 1933, in *Self-Portrait*.

28. "Love for Love: The Life and Work of St. Teresa of Jesus," in *Hidden Life*, 29.

29. Letter no. 287, to Mother Petra Brüning, December 9, 1938, in *Self-Portrait*.

30. Letter no. 296, to Mother Ottilia Thannisch, March 26, 1939, in *Self-Portrait*.

31. In 614, the Persians burned the Church of the Resurrection in Jerusalem and stole the Holy Cross.

32. "Elevation of the Cross, September 14, 1939: *Ave Crux, Spes Unica!*," in *Hidden Life*, 94.

33. Ibid.

34. Ibid., 95.

35. Letter no. 314, to Mother Johanna van Weersth, July 10, 1940, in *Self-Portrait*.

36. "The Hidden Life and Epiphany," in *Hidden Life*, 111.

37. Ibid.

38. "The Marriage of the Lamb, for September 14, 1940," in *Hidden Life*, 99.

39. Letter no. 316, to Mother Johanna van Weersth, November 17, 1940, in *Self-Portrait*.

40. Letter no. 330, to Mother Ambrosia Antonia Engelmann, December 1941, in *Self-Portrait*.

41. Letter no. 328, to Mother Johanna van Weersth, November 18, 1941, in *Self-Portrait*.

42. Letter no. 336, to Sr. Maria Ernst, April 9, 1942, in *Self-Portrait*.

43. *Science of the Cross*, 9–10.

44. Ibid., 32–33.

45. *Edith Stein*, 197–198. See also letter no. 331, to Hilde Verene Borsinger, December 31, 1941, in *Self-Portrait*.

46. "Love of the Cross: Some Thoughts for the Feast of St. John of the Cross," in *Hidden Life*, 91.

47. Ibid.

48. *Edith Stein*, 209. Some Protestants were also arrested, but most were quickly released.

49. "Exaltation of the Cross: September 14, 1941," in *Hidden Life*, 103.

50. Letter no. 57, to Sr. Adelgundis Jaegerschmid, presumably July 1930, in *Self-Portrait*.

51. "Exaltation of the Cross: September 14, 1941," in *Hidden Life*, 102.

52. "The Marriage of the Lamb, September 14, 1940," in *Hidden Life*, 100.

53. "Aphorisms in the Month of June," in *Edith Stein: Selected Writings* (Springfield, IL: Templegate, 1990), 79.

54. See testimony of Frau Bromberg in Waltraud Herbstrith, *Edith Stein* (San Francisco: Ignatius Press, 1992), 183, citing Teresia Renata Posselt, *Edith Stein: Eine Grosse Frau unseres Jahurhunderts*, 9th. ed. (Frieburg-Basel-Vienna: Herder, 1963), 178.

55. *Edith Stein*, 216.

56. Ibid., 214.

57. Ibid., 84.

58. See *Edith Stein*, 217.

59. "The Spirit of St. Elizabeth as It Informed Her Life," in *Hidden Life*, 21.

60. Letter no. 316, to Mother Johanna van Weersth, November 17, 1940, in *Self-Portrait*.

61. *Science of the Cross*, 18.

62. "Problems of Women's Education," in *Woman*, 227–28.

63. "Love of the Cross: Some Thoughts for the Feast of St. John of the Cross," in *Hidden Life*, 92–93.

64. "The Marriage of the Lamb, for September 14, 1940," in *Hidden Life*, 101.

65. "Spirituality of the Christian Woman," in *Woman*, 126.

66. *Science of the Cross*, 29.

67. Letter no. 278, to Sr. Agnella Stadtmüller, October 20, 1938, in *Self-Portrait*.

68. Letter no. 340, to Mother Ambrosia Antonia Engelmann, August 4, 1942, in *Self-Portrait.*

69. Letter no. 342, to Mother Ambrosia Antonia Engelmann, August 6, 1942, in *Self-Portrait.*

70. "Principles of Women's Education," in *Woman,* 143–144.

71. See Edith Stein, *Mystery of Christmas,* translation of *Das Weihnachtsgeheimnis* by Josephine Rucker (Darlington, England: Carmelite Press, 1985).

72. *Finite and Eternal Being,* 59.

73. Ibid.

74. "The Hidden Life and Epiphany," in *Hidden Life,* 111.

75. Letter no. 52, to Sr. Adelgundis Jaegerschmid, February 16, 1930, in *Self-Portrait.*

76. "For the First Profession of Sr. Miriam of Little St. Thérèse," in *Hidden Life,* 108.

Epilogue:
Edith Stein's Message for Today

1. *Edith Stein,* 218.

2. Ibid., 223.

3. *Life,* 216.

4. Letter no. 252, to Hedwig Dülberg, December 4, 1937, in *Self-Portrait.*

5. "The Spirit of St. Elizabeth as It Informed Her Life," in *Hidden Life,* 19.

6. The expression, "Easter in us" is from Gerard Manley Hopkins. The prayer is mine, inspired by a homily delivered by Monsignor Ronald Rozniak, pastor, Church of Our Lady of Mount Carmel, Ridgewood, NJ, April 2007.

Bibliography

Avila, Teresa of. *The Collected Works of St. Teresa of Avila.* Trans. Kieran Kavanaugh and Otilio Rodriguez. Vol. 1. 2nd ed. Washington, DC: Institute of Carmelite Studies, 1987.

Batzdorff, Susanne. *Aunt Edith: The Jewish Heritage of a Catholic Saint.* Springfield, IL: Templegate, 1998. 2nd ed, 2003.

―――. *Edith Stein: Selected Writings, with Comments, Reminiscences, and Translations of Her Prayers and Poems.* Springfield, IL: Templegate, 1990.

Borden, Sarah. *Edith Stein.* New York: Continuum, 2003.

Dougherty, Jude P. "Edith Stein's Conversion," *Crisis* 10.11 (December 1992): 41.

Fabrégues, Jean de. *Edith Stein: Philosopher, Carmelite Nun, Holocaust Martyr.* Trans. Donald M. Antoine. Boston: St. Paul Books & Media, 1993.

Graef, Hilda C. *The Scholar and the Cross: The Life and Work of Edith Stein.* Westminster, MD: Newman, 1955.

Herbstrith, Waltraud. *Edith Stein: A Biography.* Trans. Bernard Bonowitz. San Francisco: Ignatius Press, 1992.

―――. *Never Forget: Christian and Jewish Perspectives on Edith Stein.* Edited by Waltraud Herbstrith. Trans. Susanne Batzdorff. Vol. VII of *Carmelite Studies,* Steven Payne, gen. ed. Washington, DC: Institute of Carmelite Studies, 1998.

Koeppel, Josephine. *Edith Stein: Philosopher and Mystic.* Vol. 12 of *The Way of the Christian Mystics.* Gen. ed. Noel Dermot O'Donoghue. Collegeville, MN: Liturgical Press, 1990.

Neyer, Maria Amata. *Edith Stein: Her Life in Photos and Documents.* Trans. Waltraut Stein. Washington, DC: Institute of Carmelite Studies, 1999. Trans of *Edith Stein: Ihr Leben in Dokumenten und Bildern.* Würzburg: Echter Verlag, 1997.

Posselt, Teresia Renata. *Edith Stein: The Life of a Philosopher and Carmelite.* Edited by Susanne Batzdorff, Josephine Koeppel, and John Sullivan. Washington, DC: Institute for Carmelite Studies, 2005.

Scaperlanda, María Ruiz. *Edith Stein: St. Teresa Benedicta of the Cross.* Huntington, IN: Our Sunday Visitor, 2001.

Stein, Edith. *Essays on Woman.* Trans. Freda Mary Oben. 2nd ed. Vol. II of *The Collected Works of Edith Stein.* Ed. L. Gelber and Romaeus Leuven. Washington, DC: Institute of Carmelite Studies, 1996.

———. *Finite and Eternal Being.* Trans. Kurt F. Reinhardt. Vol. IX of *The Collected Works of Edith Stein.* Ed. L. Gelber and Romaeus Leuven. Washington, DC: ICS Publications, 2002.

———. *The Hidden Life: Essays, Meditations, and Spiritual Texts.* Trans. Waltraut Stein. Vol. IV of *The Collected Works of Edith Stein.* Ed. L. Gelber and Romaeus Leuven. Washington, DC: Institute of Carmelite Studies, 1992.

———. *Knowledge and Faith.* Trans. Walter Redmond. Vol. VIII of *The Collected Works of Edith Stein.* Ed. L. Gelber and Romaeus Leuven. Wash-ington, DC: Institute of Carmelite Studies, 2000.

———. *Life in a Jewish Family: 1891–1916.* Trans. Josephine Koeppel. Vol. I of *The Collected Works of Edith Stein.* Ed. L. Gelber and Romaeus Leuven. Washington, DC: Institute of Carmelite Studies, 1986.

———. *Mystery of Christmas.* Trans. Josephine Rucker. Darlington, England: Carmelite Press, 1985.

———. *On the Problem of Empathy.* Trans. Waltraut Stein. 3rd rev. ed. Vol. III of *The Collected Works of Edith Stein.* Ed. L. Gelber and Romaeus Leuven. Washinton, DC: Institute of Carmelite Studies, 1989.

———. *Philosophy of Psychology and the Humanities.* Trans. Mary Catherine Baseheart and Marianne Sawicki. Vol. VII of *The Collected Works of Edith Stein.* Ed. L. Gelber and Romaeus Leuven. Washington, DC: Institute of Carmelite Studies, 2000.

———. *The Science of the Cross.* Trans. Josephine Koeppel. Vol. VI of *The Collected Works of Edith Stein.* Ed. L. Gelber and Romaeus Leuven. Washington, DC: Institute of Carmelite Studies, 2003.

———. *Self-Portrait in Letters, 1916–1942.* Trans. Josephine Koeppel. Vol. V of *The Collected Works of Edith Stein.* Ed. L. Gelber and Romaeus Leuven. Washington, DC: Institute of Carmelite Studies, 1993.

———. *Writings of Edith Stein.* Translated by Hilda Graef. Westminster, MD: Newman, 1956.

Sullivan, John, ed. *Carmelite Studies IV: Edith Stein Symposium: Teresian Culture.* Proc. of Catholic University Symposium: "The Life and Thought of Edith Stein." September 21–22, 1984. Washington, DC: Institute of Carmelite Studies, 1987.

———. *Edith Stein: Essential Writings.* Maryknoll, NY: Orbis Books, 2002.

———. *Holiness Befits Your House: Canonization of Edith Stein, A Documentation.* Washington, DC: Institute of Carmelite Studies, 1999.

auline
BOOKS & MEDIA

A mission of the Daughters of St. Paul

As apostles of Jesus Christ,
evangelizing today's world:

We are CALLED to holiness
by God's living Word and Eucharist.

We COMMUNICATE the Gospel message
through our lives and through all
available forms of media.

We SERVE the Church
by responding to the hopes and needs
of all people with the Word of God,
in the spirit of St. Paul.

*For more information visit our Web site,
www.pauline.org.*

BOOKS & MEDIA

The Daughters of St. Paul operate book and media centers at the following addresses. Visit, call, or write the one nearest you today, or find us at www.pauline.org.

CALIFORNIA

3908 Sepulveda Blvd, Culver City, CA 90230	310-397-8676
935 Brewster Avenue, Redwood City, CA 94063	650-369-4230
5945 Balboa Avenue, San Diego, CA 92111	858-565-9181

FLORIDA

145 S.W. 107th Avenue, Miami, FL 33174	305-559-6715

HAWAII

1143 Bishop Street, Honolulu, HI 96813	808-521-2731

ILLINOIS

172 North Michigan Avenue, Chicago, IL 60601	312-346-4228

LOUISIANA

4403 Veterans Memorial Blvd, Metairie, LA 70006	504-887-7631

MASSACHUSETTS

885 Providence Hwy, Dedham, MA 02026	781-326-5385

MISSOURI

9804 Watson Road, St. Louis, MO 63126	314-965-3512

NEW YORK

64 W. 38th Street, New York, NY 10018	212-754-1110

SOUTH CAROLINA

243 King Street, Charleston, SC 29401	843-577-0175

TEXAS

Currently no book center; for parish exhibits or outreach evangelization, contact: 210–488–4123 or SanAntonio@paulinemedia.com

VIRGINIA

1025 King Street, Alexandria, VA 22314	703-549-3806

CANADA

3022 Dufferin Street, Toronto, ON M6B 3T5	416-781-9131

¡También somos su fuente para libros,
videos y música en español!